Truck Drivers in America

Truck Drivers in America

D. Daryl Wyckoff
Harvard University

Lexington Books
D. C. Heath and Company
Lexington, Massachusetts
Toronto

Library of Congress Cataloging in Publication Data

Wyckoff, D. Daryl.
  Truck drivers in America.

    1.   Motor-truck drivers—United States. I.   Title.
HD8039.M7952U58   331.7′61′3883240973   78–24793
ISBN 0–669–02818–5

Published simultaneously in Canada.

Printed in the United States of America.

International Standard Book Number: 0–669–02818–5

Library of Congress Catalog Card Number: 78–24793

10-4

Contents

List of Figures and Tables

Preface

I have been involved in academic research in the motor-carrier industry for several years. During this period I have been impressed by three observations. First, relatively little formal research has been devoted to the truck drivers compared with the vast investment in research on equipment, fuel utilization, cost structure, dispatching, information systems, and other subjects. Second, much of the little research on drivers that has been done has focused on accidents or driver error. Third, when attention has been devoted to drivers, it has been mostly situational: war stories of relatively few drivers who may have been inclined to romanticize or exaggerate their descriptions of their situations.

I set out to look at the drivers in a different way. I wanted to build a data base of the experiences of thousands of drivers so I might compare conditions or views of drivers of several different parts of the industry. The questionnaire approach I used had several advantages that I believe outweighed the disadvantages. The answers would be structured to permit the use of conventional quantitative analysis. Drivers could be completely anonymous in their responses, which I hoped would encourage candor. But, the disadvantages were not trivial. The anonymous response meant that I could not know who had completed the questionnaire. Were the respondents serious and sincere? Was some organization attempting to bias the results? Because of this concern, I took several safeguards, which are described in appendix B, to give me a high degree of confidence. But I cannot say with absolute confidence that there was not some potential for error.

The approach in this book may appear to be rather statistical and not very narrative. That is intentional. It is my purpose to present the data directly to the reader in tabular form. This will allow each reader to examine and form conclusions. My narrative is included to offer an explanation of the data and supplementary observations that stem from the drivers' comments. I have also offered my personal interpretation of some of the data, but I did so with some concern. I feel it is a responsibility to offer such an interpretation, but I believe my greater mission is to share these data with readers who are concerned with the motor-carrier industry. I hope that the availability of these data will stimulate new thinking and additional research.

My primary objective was to develop a descriptive study to report the views of truck drivers on several issues. However, certain questions had concerned me for a long time. In the process of this study, I think I found the answers. These questions included the following:

1. How do drivers view their working conditions, standards of living, and equipment?

2. Are drivers different from other workers relative to age, health, formal training, and attitudes?

3. Do owner-operator drivers have different health, experience, or driving profiles than other drivers?

4. Are there distinct differences in the attitudes, behavior, and performance of drivers who handle different commodities?

5. How high is the incidence of the use of drugs, pep pills, alcohol, and other substances while driving?

6. Do drivers who operate outside economic regulation have different records of safety compliance and accidents?

I am not sure I have fully answered these questions to my own satisfaction. Perhaps the study has raised as many questions as it answered.

This book is quantitatively oriented. That does not mean that I have not talked to drivers or ignored their letters and comments. These conversations and remarks are what explained the meaning of the numbers to me. Above all, I do not want to suggest that the drivers are simply statistics to me. The interesting stories and comments of the many drivers who took time to share them are the real lifeblood of this work. It is just that numbers tell stories, too, and sometimes that is what is needed.

I hope that this pioneering effort will serve other researches by providing data that were not available before. My greatest hope is that this work will stimulate a healthy interest in the professional truck driver as a vital member of American industry.

Acknowledgments

This book is the result of thousands of truck drivers sharing their views with me. It is only proper that they be acknowledged first. Without their participation and candor there would be nothing. Over 13,000 drivers participated. I estimate that it required a driver half an hour to complete the questionnaire. I highly respect this contribution of approxmately 6,500 hours of valuable time. I hope that this book serves them well and improves everyone's understanding of the truck drivers' jobs, aspirations, and working conditions.

Appendix B includes a detailed description of the roles of several organizations that contributed financial support of the out-of-pocket cost of distribution, collection, processing, and computer analysis of the 65,000 questionnaires that were the foundation of the research reported here. While several of these organizations had quite different views, they all shared an intense common interest in the drivers. These organizations included the Regular Common Carrier Conference of the American Trucking Associations, Inc., Union 76 Truckstops, Association of American Railroads, International Brotherhood of Teamsters, and Trucking Activities Inc.

In particular, I wish to thank Edward Moritz, Norman Weintraub, and Edward Wheeler. I gratefully acknowledge their support in this research, but hasten to add that all the analyses and conclusions included here are my own and should not be interpreted as endorsed by these groups. Besides financial support, the broad participation by groups of such diverse interest ensured that no one group could attempt to influence the outcome. Continuous monitoring by the sponsors provided a vigilance that was most welcome. Many of my observations and conclusions are directly critical of one or more of the sponsoring organizations. It is a credit to these groups that they have accepted these criticisms in the spirit in which they were offered. Specifically, they are intended to improve the lives and working conditions of the truck driver in the United States.

Andrea Truax has provided patient secretarial support to the project during the many long months. Her work included typing from the first version of the questionnaire to the final draft of this book.

Richard Hornbeck served as my research assistant in preparing the computer processing of the data. His careful and painstaking work ensured the accuracy of the data.

Ann Attridge of Marblehead, Massachusetts, spent hundreds of hours coding and examining questionnaires as part of the data processing. Her interest in the project was most valuable, and I am sorry that she did not live to see the final results of her efforts. She was a dear friend who is missed.

The UPS Foundation has long supported transportation research at Harvard University. This support, as well as the support of many scholars and researchers throughout the United States and Canada, has been vital to many transportation programs at universities. I personally wish to thank the foundation for its continued interest in my research.

Valerie, Michele, and Abigail, my wife and daughters, were all active participants in the research process. Hours were spent by every member of the family. I well remember evenings and weekends of addressing, stamping, and then opening never-ending stacks of envelopes. Sorting and reading questionnaires became a major winter occupation in our home. I thank them for their help and encouragement during the months of the process.

I wish to express my appreciation to Dean Lawrence Fouraker of the Harvard Business School for providing the resources and opportunity to write this book, even when some pressure groups attempted to suppress its publication.

Finally, I gratefully acknowledge the contributions of these people and organizations, as well as the many people who are not specifically mentioned here. I accept full responsibility for any errors or omissions that may have occurred, and I wish to emphasize that the observations and conclusions are mine.

Truck Drivers in America

1 Introduction

Truck drivers form one of the largest indirectly supervised workforces in the United States. The earnings of this workforce, particularly the portion who are members of the International Brotherhood of Teamsters, often set the pace and pattern for wage settlements for many sectors of organized labor. A powerful labor force and an integral part of a basic industry of the United States, the professional intercity truck drivers have been alternately ignored, romanticized, and criticized.

Because of the freedom of operation that truck drivers have, their attitudes and perceptions are critical since these attitudes strongly influence their behavior and performance on the road. This behavior impacts many business enterprises directly and indirectly. And, more importantly, the drivers' behavior impacts the general public with whom they share the nation's highways.

So an understanding of the truck driver is important to the general public, government, and business. This book reports the perceptions and views of a large cross section of the United States' professional intercity truck drivers and reports these drivers' performance in a candid, "unofficial" way. The views reported are the drivers' subjective opinions about subjects ranging from rather abstract, indefinite points to fairly specific, directly observable facts.

The anonymous approach to the drivers (elected in order to deal with sensitive questions) placed certain limitations on the methodology. I was unable to use certain standard statistical methods to follow up some respondents. The freeform responses could cause some bias, and I have no way to demonstrate that the drivers who failed to respond would not have different answers to the questions from those who did. Likewise, I have no way to prove that the thousands of questionnaires I received were not simply the product of a conspiracy of cynical drivers who set out to bias the study. Some internal checks between questions were used for editing purposes, but these only test for consistency of answers within a questionnaire.

I think that the real test comes from judging the credibility and balance of the answers. Few drivers seemed to find their situations simply all good or all bad. Drivers who were supportive of their employers on one score were perfectly comfortable being critical on another score. The same was true of their attitudes about their safety practices and union relationships. In my view, this candor really validates the responses in a practical way.

This book examines many aspects of the professional intercity truck driver in the United States. The attitudes and behavior of drivers under different conditions and in various subindustries within the motor-carrier industry will be compared. It is necessary to establish a common vocabulary and view of the structure of the industry to make such comparisons. The following sections provide the framework for this discussion.

Structure of the Motor-Carrier Industry

The motor-carrier industry may be described as a group of transportation subindustries that use trucks as the primary means of line-haul transportation.[1] This book focuses on the intercity drivers who perform this line-haul transportation. I realize this ignores a large and important group of drivers who perform local pickup and delivery operations. However, I feel that the greatest differences occur between the various groups of intercity drivers.

It is important for the reader to fully understand the structure of the industry and the relationship of the individual subindustries when reading the following chapters because of the comparisons that will be made. Figure 1-1 is a graphic representation of the relationship of the components of the industry.

The first basis for classification of the industry is the distinction between for-hire carriers who carry others' goods and private carriers who carry their own goods. Private carriers are exempt from regulation of the Interstate Commerce Commission (ICC), but they are also prohibited from acting as a for-hire carrier of regulated commodities. These carriers provide 40 to 60 percent of the U.S. motor-carrier intercity ton-miles.

The services of intrastate carriers are also exempted from ICC regulation. However, it should be noted that an interstate carrier may also be an intrastate carrier. Some states allow private carriers to act as a for-hire intrastate carrier. While intrastate operations fall outside the control of the ICC, they are usually controlled by a state regulatory body. The degree of the regulatory policy varies from state to state.

The rest of this discussion will focus on the interstate, for-hire carriers. A substantial group of interstate operators fall outside the economic regulation of the ICC because they transport "exempt commodities." The commodities explicitly excluded from regulation are primarily agricultural products but include some other items.[2] These exempt commodities represent between 10 and 20 percent of the U.S. motor-carrier intercity ton-miles carried. Because of the types of commodities, the exempt operations are almost entirely truckload quantities. There are often seasonal shifts in the origins of many of these commodities. Likewise, there are rather substantial seasonal fluctuations in the volume of traffic to be handled. Thus, fixed bases of operation may not be practical (or necessary).

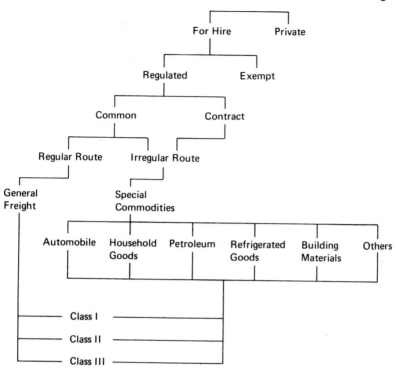

Figure 1-1. The Structure of the Interstate Motor-Carrier Industry

The federally regulated segment of the industry performs approximately 50 to 60 percent of the U.S. motor-carrier intercity ton-miles. This segment is divided into contract carriers and common carriers.

Contract carriers are a special type of regulated, for-hire carriers that are restricted to serving a limited number of specified customers in a well-defined contractual arrangement approved by the ICC. In the past, the ICC, by practice, had limited the contracts to eight to ten per carrier, which has recently been relaxed. Also now opportunities are available to contract carriers to operate also as a common carrier, a practice called "mixed operations."

Common carriers, in contrast to contract carriers, are required to offer their services equally to all shippers and are not permitted to refuse a customer who is prepared to pay the published rate for the service. This requirement is known as a common-carrier obligation.

The common-carrier group is further informally divided into regular-route and irregular-route carriers of general commodities and a variety of carriers handling special commodities, including household goods, heavy machinery, petroleum and liquid chemicals, refrigerated products (regulated portion), agricultural products (regulated portion), motor vehicles, and others.

The regular-route carriers provide service between specific points over fixed routes. Irregular-route carriers serve general areas. Carriers that operate irregular-route service generally minimize terminal (consolidation) operations and concentrate on truckload (TL) traffic—shipments from one shipper to one consignee large enough to fill, or nearly fill, one trailer. The ICC has defined these shipments as over 10,000 pounds. Of course, with modern equipment and load capacities, this would represent only one quarter of the full load of most intercity trailers. Regular-route operators typically also handle less-than-truckload (LTL) shipments. The assembly of LTL shipments into economical, intercity movement lots is done at "terminal" facilities at fixed locations and generally implies a pickup and delivery service for shipments of LTL size. The special-commodities carriers (who are generally irregular-route carriers) are primarily truckload operators.

Owner-Operators

Most of the freight carried by U.S. motor carriers is carried by drivers who are employees of companies. However, it is estimated that 25 to 40 percent of the intercity truck transportation in the United States is carried by approximately 100,000 owner-operators who drive their own trucks. These owner-operators may legally carry exempt commodities. They may also carry regulated commodities as a subcontractor of a regulated carrier. This subcontracting may be done under a long-term lease (of at least 30 days) or a trip lease which is intended to return the owner-operator to her or his home base.

Owner-operators are paid for their services in a variety of ways. While some owner-operators in the regulated industry are paid mileage or hourly rates, or flat fees for a trip, most are paid a portion of the amount charged the shipper under the published ICC-approved rate.

In theory, it is illegal for an owner-operator to carry ICC-regulated goods as a subcontractor to a private carrier. If the owner-operator does not hold the ICC authority to perform such transportation, such carriage is clearly an attempt to avoid regulation as a for-hire carrier. If the owner-operator does hold such authority, then she or he is technically acting as a primary ICC for-hire carrier rather than as a subcontractor to a private carrier.

The owner-operator, by my definition, is operating her or his own tractor truck and may also be operating her or his own trailer. A new tractor may represent an investment of over $30,000. Assuming even the most liberal downpayment practices, the owner-operator has a personal investment of several thousand dollars in equipment and debt obligations. These commitments are far different from those of a company driver who simply acts as an employee.

Nature of ICC Regulation of the Motor-Carrier Industry

Regulation of competition has usually been justified as a substitute for the free market to promote economic efficiency or some goal of income distribution. It generally has had one or more of the following purposes:

1. To prevent unreasonable prices and earnings in situations where technological and demand conditions create natural monopolies.
2. To prevent discrimination among groups with unequal bargaining power.
3. To maintain certain types of services considered to be in the public interest.
4. To ensure sufficient profits for the development and expansion of an industry in situations where competition and large differences between average total and average variable or marginal costs make it profitable to cut rates to the floor of variable costs and thus foster rate wars and instability.[3]

Railroads came under ICC regulation of rates, entry, exit, and finances through a progression of amendments to the original 1887 Interstate Commerce Act. By the 1930s it became clear that some action had to be taken to control the competitive impact of the emerging motor carriers on the railroads and reduce the intensity of price competition and rate instability that had emerged in the motor-carrier industry. The Motor Carrier Act of 1935 was the first step in the process that has brought ICC regulation of motor carriers to the present level.

As described earlier, the ICC regulates entry and exit from the industry. This takes the form of issuing certificates of public convenience and necessity to make services available to shippers. These certificates, or operating authorities, usually describe the routes or areas to be served and the commodities to be carried. Such certificates are granted by the ICC only if it can be demonstrated that there are unsatisfied public needs for the services to be performed, and that the applicant is fit, willing, and able to perform them.

Most rates of the regulated motor carriers are established through regional rate bureaus (which are carrier organizations) under the supervision of the ICC. Proposals for changing these rates are made by carriers to the rate bureau to which they belong. After hearings are held at which carriers and shippers may present arguments, the bureau then files the tariff (printed statement of the rate) and justification statements with the ICC, where they are subject to further examination. Individual carriers may take independent action outside the rate bureau, but most rates are filed in the manner just described.

The ICC generally tests rate applications in view of its evaluation of whether the proposed rates are "compensatory" and "reasonable" in view of competition. Rates must be high enough to ensure compensation of costs as based on ICC formulas, but not so high as to yield unreasonable profit to the average carrier. Although an inefficient carrier is not necessarily assured a profit, an efficient carrier may realize a very attractive profit as the result of industrywide, rather than company-by-company, regulation.

Safety Regulation

The regulation of safety comes under the U.S. Department of Transportation, Bureau of Motor Carrier Safety (BMCS). Working with various state and local authorities, the BMCS is concerned with the enforcement of compliance with federal regulations concerning equipment safety, medical examinations of drivers, log books (showing hours of service), and driving-duty hours. The following chapters frequently refer to this form of regulation because of its direct impact on the driver. Simply stated, drivers in interstate commerce are required to maintain a log book in a prescribed manner showing their activities. Naturally, misrepresentations and the use of multiple log books for any reason, but particularly for the purpose of avoiding the hours-of-service rules, are specifically illegal acts. While the rules pertaining to allowable hours of service are fairly technical and complex, simply stated, a driver has a 10-hour driving limit per day. For this reason, most drivers refer to the hours of service as the "10-hour driving limit."

Labor Organizations

Organized labor in the motor-carrier industry is primarily represented by the International Brotherhood of Teamsters (IBT). While there are some other organizations who represent drivers, particularly owner-operators, the IBT is clearly the dominant labor organization. For all practical purposes, when I refer to union membership in this book, I generally mean IBT membership.

The IBT is well known for its aggressive negotiations. The freight agreement is an industrywide bargained contract with locally ratified supplements pertaining to specific areas of subindustry situations. These contracts are negotiated on a three-year cycle.

Although the IBT has been very aggressive in pressing for wages and welfare benefits, settlements have tended to be liberal in regard to work rules and operating flexibility. Some benefits, such as cab air conditioning and allowances for lodging, are typical of the types of work condition issues negotiated by the IBT. Some groups within the IBT, such as the Professional Drivers Council (PROD), argue that greater attention should be given to explicit safety considerations. PROD, a group with the stated purpose of "Teamster reform," believes that the union should take a stronger role in promoting stronger enforcement of regulations to promote safety in the industry.

The main focus of the IBT has been organizing and promoting the interests of *employees* in the trucking industry. There is an argument about whether owner-operators are technically employees (and therefore part of the bargaining unit) of independent subcontractors.[4] The IBT has created a special owner-operator contract to accommodate such drivers in companies the drivers have organized. Also, some owner-operators maintain their own IBT membership even though they do not operate for an organized carrier. In either case, there is some evidence that these owner-operators, as a group, do not appear to identify as strongly with the IBT as do company drivers.

There are several other owner-operator groups who represent their members in various ways. One such group is the Fraternal Association of Steel Haulers (FASH), based in Pittsburgh. As the name implies, the members of this organization are primarily engaged in hauling iron and steel. FASH is attempting to establish itself as the bargaining agent for these owner-operators, many of whom are also represented by the IBT.[5]

Summary

The motor-carrier industry is a complex mosaic of subindustries that resemble one another but have their own distinctions. These subindustries are often categorized by regulatory boundaries and commodity characteristics. To understand the behavior of drivers in the trucking industry, it is necessary to disaggregate the response to this level.

Also, there are two distinctly different driver groups: company drivers and owner-operators. The first are employees. The second operate for the company in a unique fashion that falls between the status of an employee and that of an independent subcontractor. The commitments, objectives, and pressures of these owner-operators are quite different from those of an employee.

Finally, the industry is substantially represented by the Teamsters. However, a significant portion of the industry is not organized, and there are many nonunion intercity drivers on the road.

Notes

1. Substantial portions of this section are based on materials extracted from D. Daryl Wyckoff and David H. Maister, *The Motor-Carrier Industry* (Lexington, Mass.: Lexington Books, D.C. Heath, 1977).

2. For a discussion of this issue, see D. Daryl Wyckoff and David H. Maister, *The Owner-Operator: Independent Trucker* (Lexington, Mass.: Lexington Books, D.C. Heath, 1975), app. B.

3. John R. Meyers et al., *The Economics of Competition in the Transportation Industries* (Cambridge, Mass.: Harvard University Press, 1959), p. 11.

4. Wyckoff and Maister, *Owner-Operator*, chap. 6.

5. Ibid. chap. 5.

2

Drivers' Ages and Physical Conditions

In this chapter I will examine the most basic physical descriptions of the truck driver—age and physical condition. It is important to begin a discussion of the truck driver in this way because many of the drivers' attitudes and practices must be discussed with this as background material.

Perceptions of Standard of Living and Company Attitude

Are there distinct differences in the ages of drivers working in each segment of the trucking industry? I had frequently heard this issue discussed among drivers and managers. The conventional wisdom was not consistent and was often confused. I heard that the exempt drivers were young. Also, I had heard that owner-operators were older and more experienced. This raised some questions, since many exempt drivers are owner-operators. I had heard that common carriers tended to employ older drivers.

The survey cleared up these questions. Table 2-1 supports the observation that exempt drivers are younger than common-carrier drivers. The common-carrier company drivers are significantly older than any other group reported in table 2-1. A comparison of the owner-operators and company drivers operating for common carriers is useful. It supports the contention held by many drivers that the only way a young driver can join a common carrier is to be an owner-operator. The argument that common carriers only want the more responsible, older drivers may fall apart here. What may be occurring is that the seniority system, stemming from either union or company practices, tends to fill the ranks with older drivers who simply do not want to leave and thus limits the hiring of younger drivers. Or companies may show greater concern about those who drive the company-owned equipment.

Demographics

There are some age-related patterns to the attitudes of drivers concerning their standard of living and the attitude of their company concerning the drivers' welfare and working conditions. By "standard of living," it was clear that drivers meant that this was a comparison of their actual income and their personal expectations based on a complex combination of effort expended, demands, and

9

Table 2-1
Age of Drivers,
Reported by Type of Operation and Regulatory Status
(percent)

Driver's Age	Company Drivers				Owner-Operators			
	Exempt	Private	Contract	Common	Exempt	Private	Contract	Common
<25	16.85	5.80	4.80	0.79	11.00	NA	9.58	7.63
25–34	37.08	36.20	29.02	18.56	31.00	NA	35.46	28.25
35–44	33.71	35.50	30.48	31.90	33.00	NA	29.92	32.48
45–54	8.99	17.40	26.72	35.70	20.00	NA	18.82	22.46
>55	3.37	5.10	8.98	13.05	5.00	NA	6.22	9.18
Total	100.00	100.00	100.00	100.00	100.00	NA	100.00	100.00

qualifications. Older company drivers are generally more satisfied with their standard of living from driving. (See table 2-2.) The younger owner-operators are slightly more likely to indicate that they believe they make an above-average standard of living. However, the attitudes of most owner-operators appear to be less age-related. One explanation that fits this observation is that better choices of runs are available to be bid for by the senior company drivers. This appears to be a reasonable explanation; most companies have some form of bidding procedure to allocate runs among drivers. Most of these bidding systems, in either union or nonunion companies, are based to some degree on seniority of employment. However, this is not to say that age seniority is identical to company employment seniority. Also, the amount of income derived from one run compared to others available in the same company should not be so remarkably different. If there is great disparity in runs, the drivers themselves will probably rebel.

I believe that the senior company drivers simply have different perceptions and expectations based on their earnings in the past. The younger company drivers appear to have higher expectations. The younger owner-operators may be reflecting the excitement of being an independent business, and they may be confused by the appearance of high income produced by the high gross income collected rather than the net income produced after expenses are paid.

It was suggested by several truckline managers that younger company drivers are harder to please. I attempted to measure this factor by determining the driver's perception of the company's attitude toward his or her "welfare and working conditions." These responses are reported for each age group in table 2-3.

The youngest and the oldest groups in table 2-3 record the highest proportion of drivers who believe their companies are "very concerned." This is mirrored by a relatively low proportion of the drivers who believe their companies have "no concern." Why does this occur? The responses suggested two substantially different but related attitudes. The young drivers commented that they were happy to have driving jobs. Given the few company drivers in this age category, this attitude is probably justified. The older drivers exhibited two attitudes. First, the comments of these drivers might be summarized by the comment, "Things are better now than in the past." So, the more positive attitude of older drivers may stem from lower expectations and their previous experiences. Second, there was some evidence that the oldest drivers, like the youngest, were relatively happy to have driving jobs.

These perceptions should suggest something about the tendency of drivers to stay with a company. Table 2-4 shows a strong tendency for drivers to have spent a good portion of their driving career with the company they are presently driving with. For example, 73.08 percent of the drivers who have been driving over 25 years have worked for their present company over 11 years. Similarly, 67.94 percent of the drivers whose driving careers have covered 11 to 25 years have worked for their present companies 6 or more years. This argues against

Table 2-2
Perceptions of Standard of Living,
Reported by Type of Operation and Age of Driver
(percent)

Driver's Age	Company Driver's Perceived Standard of Living					Owner-Operator's Perceived Standard of Living				
	Below Average	Average	Above Average	High	Total	Below Average	Average	Above Average	High	Total
<25	9.92	52.81	22.31	4.96	100.00	20.78	52.60	20.78	5.84	100.00
25–34	5.78	60.66	29.04	4.52	100.00	24.21	56.18	16.61	3.00	100.00
35–44	3.47	61.23	30.31	4.99	100.00	25.17	58.97	13.10	2.76	100.00
45–54	2.21	60.20	31.22	6.37	100.00	22.69	59.35	21.20	3.49	100.00
>55	1.45	51.24	30.58	6.40	100.00	17.14	61.14	19.43	2.29	100.00

Table 2–3
Perceptions of Company Attitude of Company Drivers,
Reported by Age of Driver
(percent)

Driver's Age	Very Concerned	Reasonably Concerned	Some Concern	No Concern	Total
<25	28.35	30.60	28.35	12.70	100.00
25–34	15.25	31.62	17.91	35.22	100.00
35–44	15.20	35.17	18.56	32.07	100.00
45–54	17.20	37.29	14.91	30.60	100.00
⩾55	23.91	39.51	11.00	25.58	100.00

Table 2–4
Seniority with Present Company,
Reported by Years of Driving Experience of Driver
(percent)

Years of Driving Experience	Years Driving with Present Company or Driving for Self					Total
	0–2	3–5	6–10	11–25	>25	
0– 2	100.00	NA	NA	NA	NA	100.00
3– 5	40.42	59.68	NA	NA	NA	100.00
6–10	26.13	35.27	38.60	NA	NA	100.00
11–25	13.62	18.44	31.23	36.71	NA	100.00
>25	4.87	8.64	13.41	44.71	28.37	100.00

the image of the free-spirited truck driver wandering from employer to employer.

Driver Training

Where do drivers learn to drive professionally? In fact, the majority of drivers have not received formal training. Since the drivers who did have formal training seldom had more than one source of such training, the sum of the proportion of drivers who received formal training under each type of age category in table 2–5 essentially represents the group who had formal training. Or, for the age

Table 2-5
Frequency of Formal Driver Training,
Reported by Type of Training and Age of Driver
(percent)

Type of Formal Driver's Training	Driver's Age				
	<25	*25–34*	*35–44*	*45–55*	*>55*
Company	31.9	13.7	9.7	7.0	7.3
Union	0.7	0.7	0.5	0.5	0.2
Armed services	4.7	6.0	6.4	5.7	7.4
Private	13.0	18.1	10.0	3.6	1.7
Other	8.6	7.4	5.7	5.0	5.2

groups reported in table 2-5, the proportions of drivers without formal training are approximately 41, 54, 68, 78, and 79 percent. Formal training of truck drivers is certainly a more recent institution. Drivers over 45 years old simply did not rely on such institutions. The large proportion (nearly 32 percent) of drivers under 25 years old who have received formal training from a company program suggests the possibility that this may have been a requirement imposed on such young drivers for entry into this profession. Many companies have turned to such training as a part of a recruitment program for company drivers and potential owner-operators. I will defer until chapter 3 the analysis of the effectiveness of this training in producing safer drivers or happier employees. However, at this point it is appropriate to consider the driving and safety practices and performance of drivers on the basis of age. I must caution the reader that simply considering such behavior on the basis of age alone may provide only part of the story because, as discussed earlier in this chapter, of the differences in ages in each segment of the industry and the practices of such companies. However, table 2-6 is useful as a first examination. Greater adherence to safety rules is seen with increased age of the driver. One older driver summarized the view of many drivers when he commented, "As you get older you don't run the risks and don't do the things you did when you were younger." However, is the older, more mature driver desirable on the basis of physical condition? This leads to the examination of the physical condition and health of drivers.

Physical Condition and Health

Conventional wisdom suggests that truck drivers are physically vigorous, rough-and-tumble people. Are truck drivers in better or poorer physical condition than

Table 2–6
Driver Safety Practices and Performance,
Reported by Age
(percent)

	Driver's Age		
Item	*<25*	*25–50*	*>50*
Cruising speed, mph	62.0	59.8	58.1
Percentage who regularly misrepresent logs	39.0	16.0	4.1
Percentage who regularly drive beyond the 10-hour limitation	36.1	12.0	2.7
Moving violations per 100,000 miles per year	1.3	0.7	0.3
Reportable accidents per 100,000 miles per year	0.4	0.2	0.2

the general population? Are truck drivers, particularly the senior drivers, in adequate physical condition to meet the demands of the work?

Table 2–7 summarizes the drivers' responses to questions regarding their physical condition. There are several complaints that definitely increase with the age group of the driver. Some of these complaints are certainly reflections of the aging process. Diabetes, back problems, ulcers, heart problems, nervous problems, and several other conditions are certainly age-related. What is interesting to note is that several complaints appear to reach a plateau in middle age and do not become more frequently reported. Examples of this are back problems, hemorrhoids, nervous conditions, and frequent headaches. I think there are three explanations for such results. First, the complaints are often self-diagnosed. Perhaps the younger drivers find that health complaints are not consistent with their own self-image. Second, it may be that some of these complaints are job-related. After several years of driving, those drivers who are most susceptible to the complaints have already experienced them. This might apply most directly to such items as frequent headaches and nervous problems. Third, it is clear that the quality of some of the work conditions has changed substantially since some of the older drivers joined the industry. Reduced lifting and better truck suspension may partly account for fewer complaints of hernias, hemorrhoids, and kidney problems among the young drivers.

It would be useful to compare the responses of the truck drivers of this study with the responses of other categories of workers and the general population. Lack of data prevents such direct comparison. However, some clues are provided from the data collected by the U.S. National Center for Health Statistics. One must be careful in comparing the data in tables 2-7 and 2-8. Table 2-7 is based on the driver's perception of his or her condition. This may be based on a physician's diagnosis, but it may also be based on subjective self-diagnosis. Also, the data in table 2-8 are based on a very specific definition of physical problems. That is, the physical problem is (1) chronic, having existed for over six months, and (2) serious enough to cause some limitation of activites. Such limitations may range from taking medication or using a corrective device to complete disability short of hospitalization or other institutionalization. Recognizing these inconsistencies in definitions, it is still interesting to make a comparison of several conditions.

Truck drivers do appear to have substantially greater hernia and back problems. Kidney and nervous problems are also more frequent. These might all well be profession-related problems. It is particularly interesting to note that the incidence of heart problems is lower than might be expected among the senior truck drivers.

Table 2-9 reports the proportion of the general population that wears corrective lenses for visual problems. This is substantially higher for every age category than that reported by the truck drivers, which may stem partly from the way the question was asked of the drivers. Specifically, they were asked if

Table 2-7
Driver's Health Problems,
Reported by Age
(percent)

	Driver's Age		
Health Problem	<25	25-50	>50
Visual	11.9	10.6	14.5
Hearing	1.7	7.0	10.0
Hernia	1.0	2.0	2.9
Back	11.2	21.0	21.6
Hemorrhoid	5.9	18.8	17.3
Ulcers	6.6	9.9	10.5
Diabetes	nil	0.7	2.8
Kidney	2.6	4.1	4.3
High blood pressure	2.6	6.3	10.5
Low blood pressure	0.3	1.0	1.2
Heart	0.7	1.1	3.0
Nervous	3.3	6.4	6.5
Varicose veins	0.7	1.9	2.8
Frequent headaches	5.0	7.5	6.4

Table 2-8
Proportion of U.S. Male Population outside Health Institutions Who Report Chronic Health Complaints Serious Enough to Cause Any Limitation of Activities, Reported by Age, 1970
(percent)

Chronic Health Complaint	Age	
	<45	45–65
Hernia	0.08	0.60
Back problems	0.60	1.86
Ulcers or stomach problems	0.17	1.06
Diabetes	0.09	0.80
Kidney problems	0.06	0.15
Hypertension	0.07	0.78
Heart problems	0.32	4.70
Nervous problems	0.27	1.00

Adapted from U.S. National Center for Health Statistics, *Vital and Health Statistics*, series 10.

Table 2-9
Proportion of U.S. Population Who Report Wearing Corrective Lenses for Visual Problems Reported by Age, 1971

Age	Proportion Who Wear Corrective Lenses[a]
17–24	40.7
25–44	42.1
≥45	88.3

Source: U.S. Center for Health Statistics. *Vital and Health Statistics*, series 10, no. 79.

[a]Excludes sunglasses worn only to filter light and safety glasses worn only for the protection of the eyes. Corrective lenses include glasses and contact lenses.

they had visual problems. This might be interpreted as vision that cannot be fully corrected with lenses. However, comments on the questionnaires suggest that most drivers interpreted this as being any visual impairment, whether fully corrected or not. Based on this latter interpretation, there is strong evidence that truck drivers do not believe they need glasses.

Table 2-10
Drivers' Health Problems,
Reported by Type of Operation and Regulatory Status
(percent)

Health Problem	Company Drivers				Owner-Operators			
	Exempt	*Private*	*Contract*	*Common*	*Exempt*	*Private*	*Contract*	*Common*
Visual	18.0	14.6	13.5	11.4	14.0	NA	11.2	11.1
Hearing	5.6	6.9	7.0	8.5	7.0	NA	4.0	5.9
Hernia	3.4	2.1	1.9	2.4	nil	NA	1.8	1.8
Back	11.2	2.5	19.5	23.1	18.0	NA	11.9	14.9
Hemorrhoid	13.5	19.9	14.3	20.1	10.0	NA	13.0	17.3
Ulcers	11.2	10.7	9.9	10.9	10.0	NA	6.8	7.6
Diabetes	nil	0.2	0.2	1.4	1.0	NA	1.2	0.6
Kidney	7.9	5.8	4.3	4.5	3.0	NA	2.7	3.1
High blood pressure	4.5	6.0	8.9	8.2	3.0	NA	4.5	5.9
Low blood pressure	2.3	2.1	1.2	0.9	1.0	NA	0.7	1.1
Heart	nil	0.7	1.7	1.8	1.0	NA	0.8	1.3
Nervous	6.7	3.7	5.2	7.5	6.0	NA	4.0	3.5
Varicose veins	1.1	2.1	2.3	2.1	nil	NA	2.7	1.4
Frequent headaches	3.4	6.7	7.9	7.8	6.0	NA	5.8	4.9

Table 2–11
Experience of Drivers Dozing or Falling Asleep at Wheel While Driving,
Reported by Age
(percent)

Experience of Dozing or Falling Asleep at Wheel in Past Year	Driver's Age		
	<25	*25–50*	*>50*
Never	26.76	29.35	43.61
Once or twice	42.14	40.28	33.40
Occasionally	28.76	28.49	22.00
Regularly	2.34	1.88	0.99
Total	100.00	100.00	100.00

Several critics of owner-operators claim that many drivers turned to this form of operation because they could not meet the standards for physical condition required for company drivers. Similar claims were made about all drivers in the exempt segments of the industry. Table 2-10 addresses these arguments.

There is no evidence in table 2-10 to support such positions. For example, if one compares the physical condition of the company drivers and owner-operators of common carriers, it might be concluded that owner-operators are in superior physical condition. The same pattern is seen, but less clearly, in the exempt and contract categories.

The differences in the physical condition of exempt owner-operators appear to be only sightly poorer than reported in other owner-operator categories. The common-carrier company drivers report more physical complaints in some categories, but this is no greater than would be expected from their age.

Finally, are older drivers less attentive or more likely to doze or fall asleep at the wheel? Table 2-11 suggests the opposite. The younger driver is over twice as likely to regularly experience this problem. Similarly, the older driver is nearly twice as likely to never experience dozing or falling asleep at the wheel. The causes of this problem are discussed in chapter 6. However, at this point, I would refer to the greater incidence of abuse of the 10-hour driving limitation by the younger drivers noted earlier in table 2-6.

Summary

The common-carriers show distinct patterns of having older employees, with a clear absence of drivers under 25 years old. Becoming an owner-operator may be one of the few ways a young driver can enter common carriage.

Older company drivers generally have more positive feelings about their standard of living. However, younger owner-operators are more positive about their standard of living in that group. Perception of company attitude is bimodal. The youngest and oldest drivers have the most positive attitudes. The net result of these perceptions is a strong tendency toward stability among drivers with the most seniority.

There is a strong trend toward a greater proportion of professional drivers to receive some formal driver training. This training is primarily provided by the trucking companies themselves. However, there is a strong representation of private training school training among the younger drivers. The armed services are a diminishing source of such training.

Finally, there is evidence that adherence to safety practices is related to age.

While truck drivers do experience increased incidence of health problems with age, the increase is not as striking as one might expect from the experience of the general population. Truck drivers appear to be in better physical condition than others of the same age in the general population as reported on the basis of physical limitations. Adherence to driving-hour limitations may account for greater attentiveness (less dozing or falling asleep at the wheel) among older drivers. Superior performance, or fewer moving violations and reportable accidents, suggests that the gains of maturity clearly offset any physical limitations from age.

3

Driver Training

How do professional intercity drivers learn their job of driving? The majority of the drivers I studied never had formal driver training. Most said that they had learned from friends or "just picked it up."

In fact, there is a great deal for a driver to learn. While most drivers who learned the trade by informal means have excellent driving records, a number of aspects of the driver's profession lend themselves to formal teaching. These are subjects that are not tied directly to physical skills such as mastering smooth shifting of the ten-speed transmission, backing or parking a tractor and trailer combination into a tight location, or braking a rig.

Subjects such as the Department of Transportation regulations and hours of service and log book regulations require specific detailed technical knowledge. These are procedures that an interstate driver must use correctly every day to comply with the law. This material lends itself to formal instruction methods. There are many specific, but basic, techniques that will increase the safety of the driver and reduce hazards to herself or himself or others on the road. These include emergency driving and defensive driving. Emergency driving includes such skills as how to control a rig in the case of loss of brakes or other failure. Defensive driving deals with anticipating problems from other drivers. These skills, when properly applied, are believed to have demonstrated benefits. Finally, there are subjects that relate to the specific characteristics of the commodities carried. These subjects might include cargo loading and securing. Of course, such subjects are commodity-specific. Another subject of this type relates to handling dangerous materials.

Sources of Formal Driver Training

There has been a trend toward a greater use of formal driver training among younger drivers. Table 3-1 summarizes the frequency of types of formal driver training by age group. It is seen that the union is not a great source of formal driver training. In fact, the national union stated that the respondents were referring to driving programs conducted by local organizations, since the union does not have a program officially endorsed or conducted at the national level. The armed forces were once an important source of formal driver training. Of course, the importance of this source is related to military activity. A strong

21

Table 3-1
Proportion of Drivers in Each Age Group
Who Have Had Formal Driver Training
(percent)

Type of Formal Driver's Training	Driver's Age				
	<25	25-34	35-44	45-55	>55
Company	31.9	13.7	9.7	7.0	7.3
Union	0.7	0.7	0.5	0.5	0.2
Armed services	4.7	6.0	6.4	5.7	7.4
Private	13.0	18.1	10.0	3.6	1.7
Other	8.6	7.4	5.7	5.0	5.2

trend toward the use of private schools can be seen, although there has been a slight downturn among the youngest drivers.

The most striking trend apparent in table 3-1 is the increasing importance of company-sponsored programs. It appears that the substantial increase in this type of training may have displaced some of the earlier popularity of private school programs.

Users of Formally Trained Drivers

Who employs these formally trained drivers? Table 3-2 reports several interesting patterns in formal training. Contrary to my own expectations, common-carrier company drivers do not show a particularly high incidence of formal training. However, this is related to the fact that these drivers are generally older, a group, as seen in table 3-1, which is less likely to have had formal training.

The drivers who have been trained in private schools appear to become company drivers in the exempt and contract segments and owner-operators working for contract carriers.

The most striking observation is the high incidence of contract-carrier owner-operators who have received formal training in company programs. It appears that there may be substantial recruiting of untrained drivers who are, in turn, trained by the contract carrier. To a lesser degree, this also appears to be the case among common-carrier owner-operators.

Training Program Effectiveness

What material is actually covered in formal training programs? I asked drivers this question. This research method has the disadvantage of depending on the

Table 3-2
Formal Driver Training,
Reported by Type of Operation and Regulatory Status
(percent)

Formal Driver Training	Company Drivers				Owner-Operators			
	Exempt	*Private*	*Contract*	*Common*	*Exempt*	*Private*	*Contract*	*Common*
Company	4.5	6.0	6.2	6.3	7.0	NA	42.1	17.6
Union	1.1	6.0	0.8	0.5	nil	NA	0.5	0.3
Armed services	11.2	7.4	7.0	5.9	1.0	NA	5.8	5.6
Private	11.2	9.7	10.6	8.8	3.0	NA	12.9	8.3
Other	5.6	6.9	8.9	5.5	5.0	NA	5.8	3.5

Table 3-3
Topics Covered in Formal Driving Programs
(percent)

Topics Covered in Formal Driving Program	Type of Formal Driving School Attended				
	Company	Union	Armed Forces	Private	Other
Information Used Daily					
Hours of service and log books	92.0	66.7	47.4	93.7	55.7
DOT safety regulations	91.3	79.2	50.0	93.2	55.1
Safe Driving Topics					
Emergency driving	45.6	64.6	58.0	52.4	37.1
Defensive driving	76.0	75.0	76.3	89.9	56.6
Commodity-Specific Topics					
Handling dangerous materials	35.5	48.0	59.0	50.8	33.7
Cargo loading and securing	70.7	54.2	60.1	40.6	31.4

driver's memory of the material covered. However, this approach has the advantage that drivers will be most likely to remember the topics which made the greatest impression on them. The results are summarized in table 3-3.

The topics which a driver is likely to use daily are well covered in company and private programs. Of course, these are subjects that have little to do with a driver in the armed forces. So, as might be expected, they are less likely to be covered in the armed forces' driver programs.

About three-quarters of the drivers remember defensive driving topics being covered in their programs. Only about half of the drivers remember emergency driving being discussed.

Commodity-specific topics such as cargo loading and securing are most likely to be dealt with in company programs. Handling hazardous materials appears to receive little attention. I found that only 12.8 percent of the drivers who said that they frequently carried hazardous materials had received appropriate formal training. This was just slightly higher than the proportion of drivers who did not carry hazardous materials.

How do drivers who have received formal training perform? One might expect that a formally trained driver would have better compliance with safety practices and have safer driving records. In fact, this is not demonstrated by the results. Drivers who received formal training in private schools and from company programs appeared, on the average, to drive faster, misrepresented their log books, exceeded the 10-hour limit more regularly, and had more accidents per 100,000 miles. Part of this poorer compliance can be explained by the fact that more young drivers had received formal training, and young drivers generally had poorer records. But this is not a complete explanation. It appears as if formal

Table 3–4
Driving Performance and Records of Drivers,
Reported by Type of Formal Driver Training

Type of Formal Driver Training	Average Cruising Speed, mph	Regularly Drive beyond 10-Hour Limit percent	Regularly Misrepresent Log percent	Reportable Accidents per 100,000 Miles
Company	59.9	14.4	18.9	0.3
Union	58.6	10.6	15.9	0.3
Armed services	59.3	9.7	13.1	0.2
Private	59.9	12.0	18.0	0.3
Other	59.9	12.0	15.3	0.2
Average of all drivers	59.4	10.2	13.5	0.2

training had built false confidence and possibly informed drivers how to abuse the law. These data raise serious questions about what formal driver training is accomplishing.

Summary

The majority of the drivers have not received formal driver training, but there is a clear trend toward greater use of such training among the younger drivers. Both private and company programs have gained popularity.

Owner-operators in the contract- and common-carrier segments are more frequently trained in company programs.

The formal training programs appear to deal heavily with Department of Transporation requirements, log book procedures, and hours-of-service regulations. They fall short in emergency and defensive driving training, and relatively few drivers who carry hazardous materials have had formal training on how to handle them.

Unfortunately, serious doubts are raised about how effective formal driver training has been. At best, the records of formally trained drivers are no worse. But there is evidence that formally trained drivers may be more likely to abuse basic operating laws related to safety, and these drivers have a higher incidence of reportable accidents.

4   Union Status

The trucking industry is well known for its strong union, the International Brotherhood of Teamsters, Chauffeurs, Warehousemen, and Helpers of America. However, there has been little in the public domain about the demographic composition of the Teamster membership and relative penetration of the union into the various segments of the trucking industry. Likewise, little has been known publicly about the attitudes of the rank-and-file Teamster members who are professional heavy-duty truck drivers.

This chapter compares behavior and attitudes of the union truck drivers with their nonunion counterparts. Age, driving record and performance, attitudes, practices, and employment turnover will be examined. In discussing the attitudes of the drivers, it must be remembered that the survey was conducted in a period almost exactly between contract negotiations that occur on a three-year cycle. So the opinions expressed are relatively free from the influence of impending negotiation.

Drivers' Ages

Union truck drivers were found to be older than nonunion truck drivers. As seen in table 4-1, very few union drivers are in the under-25 age group, while this is a fairly heavily represented age group among the nonunion drivers. Likewise, the older age groups, particularly over 45 years, are heavily union.

Several reasons for this age distribution were suggested by the drivers' individual responses. First, union structure and job bid procedures tend to favor drivers with greater seniority. Second, many of the nonunion companies are apparently more willing to hire younger drivers. Third, statements of younger nonunion drivers often implied that the union did not appeal to them because of their feelings about large organizations and their low expectations for the benefits they would derive from membership. The age of the union drivers would lead one to expect more driving experience. Table 4-2 supports this.

Table 4-1
Distribution of Age of Drivers,
Reported by Union Status
(percent)

	Union Status	
Age of Driver	*Union*	*Nonunion*
<25	1.59	10.16
25–34	19.86	36.40
35–44	32.04	30.04
45–54	33.86	16.81
>55	12.65	6.59
Total	100.00	100.00

Table 4-2
Years of Driving Experience,
Reported by Union Status
(percent)

	Union Status	
Years of Driving Experience	*Union*	*Nonunion*
0– 2	2.60	5.61
3– 5	6.49	19.34
6–10	15.42	26.60
11–25	43.98	37.24
>25	31.51	11.21
Total	100.00	100.00

Union Penetration

It is difficult to determine the true penetration of union membership among company drivers and owner-operators who carry each type of commodity. However, table 4-3 summarizes the proportion of respondents to the survey in each category. Caution must be used in considering table 4-3, since I am not sure that this constitutes a representative sample. But since there is so little information available on this subject, these data serve as an interesting insight to this question.

One cannot help but note the striking difference between union membership of company drivers and owner-operators. But this is to be expected from the highly independent personality of the owner-operators.

Table 4–3
Proportion of Drivers Who Indicated Union Membership,
Reported by Commodities Carried and Type of Operation
(percent)

	Type of Operation	
Commodities Regularly Carried This Past Year	Company Drivers	Owner-Operators
Iron and Steel	83.3	69.6
Heavy metal objects, machinery	86.4	63.6
Motor vehicles	94.6	70.6
Bulk products	84.1	a
Farm products (not refrig.)	75.1	21.9
Refrigerated	58.4	17.5
General commodities	95.5	62.7
Household goods	91.5	74.7
Building materials	85.5	39.7
Other	86.9	51.0

aSample too small to be reliable.

Safety Practices

Turning to table 4–4, we see the comparison of the driving and safety practices of union and nonunion truck drivers. Both categories of drivers are further broken down into company drivers and owner-operators. It should be noted that union company drivers are usually operating under the terms of a labor contract. Union owner-operators may be operating under a labor contract; however, this group also includes union members who are driving outside such an agreement. The union owner-operators, as a group, are substantially less firmly attached to the union. Because of their ownership of equipment, they generally see themselves as independent contractors rather than as employees.

The practices and performances of union company drivers in table 4–4 appear to be substantially safer than for any other category of driver. The next safest *practices* were found among the union owner-operators, although this group had the poorest record of reportable accidents per 100,000 miles driven per year.

Is union membership related to these better records? The answer is not clear. It may be related, but union membership is related to three other important variables. As already seen in table 4–1, union drivers are older. As disussed in chapter 3, older drivers tend to be safer. Also, the terms of the union contract and reporting procedures for payment are such that excessive hours of service and speeding are highly detectable. Finally, the union has penetrated most

Table 4-4
Driving Records and Safety Practices of
Union Drivers Compared to Nonunion Drivers

	Union		Nonunion	
Item	Company Drivers	Owner-Operators	Company Drivers	Owner-Operators
Cruising speed, mph	58.8	60.1	61.8	60.8
Percentage of drivers using multiple log books	1.6	9.1	17.3	15.4
Percentage of drivers who regularly misrepresent log books	4.8	27.9	35.7	37.8
Percentage of drivers who regularly drive beyond the 10-hour limitation	2.6	20.7	31.9	31.5
Moving violations per 100,000 miles driven per year	0.4	0.7	1.2	1.0
Reportable accidents per 100,000 miles driven per year	0.2	0.3	0.3	0.3

deeply into the segments of the industry that are most heavily regulated economically. As is discussed in chapter 10, there is a strong association between economic regulation and adherence to hours-of-service and speed limitations.

So, it is not clear how much of the credit union membership per se can take for this relatively better performance. Also, there is the question of whether this performance is satisfactory in the absolute sense. Is an average speed of 3.8 miles per hour above the national speed limit of 55 miles per hour acceptable? Is it reasonable that 2.6 percent of the drivers regularly exceed the 10-hour driving limit? The members of the Professional Drivers Council (generally referred to as PROD) do not think so. This group, with the stated purpose of "Teamster reform," strongly believes that efforts for stronger enforcement and regulation should be more aggressively led by the union.

Perceptions of Standard of Living and Company Attitude

How do members of the union see their standard of living derived from their driving income? For the purpose of this analysis I focused on company drivers. Union and nonunion owner-operators are discussed in great detail in chapter 9.

Union company drivers strongly believe that their standard of living is average or above. Only 2 percent of the union drivers stated that they believed their standard of living derived from their driving income was below average. As seen in table 4-5, the nonunion drivers had substantially different feelings about this. A full 15 percent believed their standard of living to be below average. The proportion of nonunion drivers who believed they had an above-average standard of living was significantly lower.

One might expect that employees who feel that their job provides a good standard of living would also have a positive attitude toward their employers. The measure of this attitude that I used was the driver's perception of his or her "company's attitude toward [his or her] welfare and working conditions." This question produced some remarkable results. Nonunion drivers gave their companies relatively higher marks for their concern and interest in the situation. The union drivers in table 4-5 reported perceptions of lower levels of concern shown by their employers. This same pattern holds up when the analysis is limited to drivers who regularly carry general commodities, the drivers who are the main group covered by the Teamster Master Freight Agreement (see table 4-6).

Table 4-5
Company Drivers' Perceptions of Standard of Living and Company Attitude toward Their Welfare and Working Conditions, Reported by Union Status
(percent)

	Union Status	
	Union	*Nonunion*
Perception of Standard of Living		
High	5.8	4.5
Above average	32.0	20.3
Average	60.2	59.7
Below average	2.0	15.5
Total	100.0	100.0
Perception of Company Attitude		
Very concerned	15.0	31.8
Reasonably concerned	36.2	33.8
Some concern	32.0	25.0
No concern	16.8	9.4
Total	100.0	100.0

Table 4-6
Perceptions of Standard of Living and Company Attitude
of Company Drivers Who Regularly Carry General Commodities,
Reported by Union Status
(percent)

	Union Status	
	Union	*Nonunion*
Perception of		
Standard of Living		
High	5.79	4.63
Above average	32.90	24.54
Average	59.71	57.87
Below average	1.60	12.96
Total	100.00	100.00
Perception of		
Company Attitude		
Very concerned	13.49	35.35
Reasonably concerned	36.42	29.74
Some concern	32.71	22.84
No concern	17.38	12.07
Total	100.00	100.00

There is a difference between how union and nonunion drivers relate standard of living and perception of their company's attitude toward them. Table 4-7 summarizes the perception of company attitude based on the driver's response on standard of living.

The union drivers showed some tendency toward equating perceptions of standard of living and company attitude. That is, union drivers who felt they had high standards of living tended to give their employers less credit for concern, while nonunion drivers who felt they had lower standards of living tended to give their employers more credit for concern. Also, the attitudes of nonunion drivers toward their employers' concerns were substantially higher, as seen in table 4-5, but also relatively less sensitive to the driver's perception of standard of living.

There are several interpretations of these results. First, union drivers are relatively content economically. To some extent, economic satisfaction does buy the employer an amount of positive driver attitude. But money is not everything. The nonunion employers get more positive reactions from their drivers despite lower standards of living.

Another explanation is that the union has tended to be most successful in organizing drivers who work for employers that have shown the least concern

Table 4–7
Company Drivers' Perceptions of Company Attitude toward
Their Welfare and Working Conditions,
Reported by Drivers' Perceptions of Standard of Living and Union Status
(percent)

	Perception of Standard of Living			
Perception of Company Attitude	*High*	*Above Average*	*Average*	*Below Average*
Union Company Drivers				
Very concerned	30.7	15.1	13.6	10.9
Reasonably concerned	36.7	38.9	35.0	25.2
Some concern	22.7	31.9	33.0	30.3
No concern	9.9	14.1	18.4	33.6
Total	100.0	100.0	100.0	100.0
Nonunion Company Drivers				
Very concerned	43.3	40.0	30.8	21.0
Reasonably concerned	36.7	34.1	35.7	25.0
Some concern	10.0	22.9	25.3	31.0
No concern	10.0	3.0	8.2	23.0
Total	100.0	100.0	100.0	100.0

for their drivers. A counterexplanation is that nonunion employers attempt to gain the favor of their drivers by showing greater incidence of concern, thus being able to pay less than they would if they were unionized. A corollary to this is an attitude of the union employer that since it pays well, it owes its employees little more. Finally, one more explanation is that the union sews seeds of hostility toward employers among its rank-and-file members.

It is difficult to judge which interpretation is most correct. Each company is a special situation which is a unique combination of the factors described. Rather than assign a cause to the attitude, I have attempted to examine the detailed attitudes of union drivers regarding several features of their work conditions.

Union drivers are substantially more critical of their "cab work conditions." Table 4-8 shows that union drivers are approximately three times as likely to find major problems in such features of their cab as noise level, vibration, fumes, seating, temperature and humidity, and cleanliness. Table 4-9 reports the drivers' attitudes toward the safety of their equipment. It appears that union drivers also hold the opinion that their equipment is less safe. The question is, Are these drivers' attitudes on those points negative because of a general perception of company attitude, or are these attitudes the by-product of the general attitude?

Table 4-8
Cab Work Conditions, Proportion of Drivers
Who Find Each Feature to Be a Major Problem,
Reported by Union Status
(percent)

	Union Status	
Item	Union	Nonunion
Noise	16.3	5.3
Vibration	21.2	7.4
Fumes	14.8	3.6
Seating	21.5	6.9
Temperature/humidity	18.6	5.9
Cleanliness	28.1	8.1

Table 4-9
Proportion of Company Drivers Who
Consider Equipment Unsafe,
Reported by Union Status
(percent)

	Union Status	
Equipment System	Union	Nonunion
Tractor		
Tires	6.9	4.1
Electrical	5.1	5.7
Brakes	17.1	8.0
Engine	12.7	5.7
Suspension	26.2	8.1
Trailer		
Tires	8.9	7.7
Electrical	6.5	10.1
Brakes	20.8	13.4
Suspension	9.3	4.8

One test of this is, Do union drivers simply complain more about everything? The answer is no. In table 4-10 it is seen that union drivers are equally or more tolerant of many aspects of their work conditions. The main differences seen in table 4-10 are in attitudes about federal and state inspections, driving hours, responsibility for cargo, loading and unloading, and unreasonable dispatches.

The nonunion drivers' greater sensitivity about federal and state inspections

Table 4-10
On-the-Road Work Conditions, Proportion of Drivers
Who Find Each Feature to Be a Major Problem,
Reported by Union Status
(percent)

	Union Status	
Item	*Union*	*Nonunion*
Monotony/boredom	6.7	7.1
Loneliness	5.5	9.9
Road conditions	22.9	25.0
Bad weather	18.3	14.4
Night driving	2.8	2.4
Other drivers	14.3	18.3
Federal and state inspections	7.3	27.1
Long driving hours	10.4	5.5
Responsibility for cargo	8.1	4.3
Loading and unloading	5.0	16.2
Unreasonable dispatches	16.3	12.9

is hardly surprising given the high incidence of misrepresented log books and driving hour limitation violations reported by this group.

It is interesting to note that the union drivers have a higher complaint about long driving hours. Tables 4-11 and 4-12 clearly show that the union drivers average fewer hours of work in a typical 7-day work week than other drivers. This apparent inconsistency may be explained by the older age and the relatively higher satisfaction with standard of living of the union drivers.

The union drivers feel a greater responsibility for their cargo. This may stem from the attitudes of the union companies. The nonunion drivers are more likely to be directly responsible for unloading. This is a substantial demand, particularly after a strenuous drive, from which the union driver is generally protected.

Finally, the union driver is more sensitive to "unreasonable dispatches."

In table 4-13, the union drivers are substantially more sensitive to lack of exercise, probably an age-related issue, and irregular hours. The question of lack of exercise and driving hours may be partially related to the larger proportion of union drivers who do not rest or rest sitting in the seat of the cab of their trucks. Table 4-14 summarizes the method of rest used by union and nonunion drivers. Over half of the union drivers do not rest or rest in the seat of their cabs. While many of these drivers are running scheduled runs or relay operations that do not require them to be away from their home base, such operations appear still to require proper rest, which will be discussed in chapter 6.

As a final note, I would like to discuss two related issues—the relationship of age and perception of company attitudes and employee turnover. Table 4-15

Table 4-11
Average Hours Worked in Typical Seven-Day
Work Week, Reported by Type of Operation
and Union Status

	Hours Worked in Typical Seven-Day Week
Union	
Company drivers	61.4
Owner-operators	67.0
Nonunion	
Company drivers	69.7
Owner-operators	70.0

Table 4-12
Distribution of Hours Worked in Typical Seven-Day Work Week,
Reported by Type of Operation and Union Status
(percent)

	Union		Nonunion	
Hours Worked in Typical Seven-Day Work Week	*Company Drivers*	*Owner-Operators*	*Company Drivers*	*Owner-Operators*
<40	1.06	2.37	1.77	2.68
40–60	28.22	23.00	20.22	21.69
61–70	40.75	28.63	25.36	24.10
>70	29.97	46.00	52.65	51.54
Total	100.00	100.00	100.00	100.00

Table 4-13
Personal Aspects of Work Conditions, Proportion of Drivers
Who Find Each Feature to Be a Major Problem,
Reported by Union Status
(percent)

	Union Status	
Item	*Union*	*Nonunion*
Separation from home	19.0	15.3
Lack of exercise	21.0	12.2
Irregular hours	26.6	9.3

shows different patterns with age regarding drivers' attitudes among union and nonunion drivers. The young union company driver is substantially less satisfied with the company's attitude. Older union drivers seem to be more satisfied (or less dissatisfied). The proportion of drivers in the "no concern" category among the nonunion drivers increases with age. What seems to occur is that the discontented union drivers become reasonably more contented with age. The doubtful ("some concern") nonunion drivers seem to shift to the ranks of the dissatisfied with age. Note that the older nonunion drivers are more extreme in their perceptions of their employers' attitudes.

I suspect these results are closely related employee turnover. As seen in table 4-16, union drivers report lower turnover. That is, a greater proportion of drivers have been with the same company longer relative to the number of years the driver has driven. I believe that the union seniority system may aggravate the younger drivers, but the older drivers are relatively more satisfied as a result of it. The nonunion drivers tend to be more mobile and seem to be looking for a more attractive situation.

Summary

Union drivers are older, more experienced drivers. They demonstrate a high tendency to stay with their employers, but this is a trait of most company drivers, despite their public image of being free spirits lightly attached to their companies.

It appears that the union company drivers demonstrate better safety practices and compliance with driving restrictions. This results in fewer moving violations and reportable accidents, although this record might be even better.

Table 4-14
How Drivers Rest While on the Road,
Reported by Union Status
(percent)

How Do You Rest on the Road?	Union Status	
	Union	Nonunion
Don't rest	22.17	10.42
Sleeper cab	18.66	70.20
Seat of cab	31.59	8.77
Motel or hotel	23.70	7.75
Rest station	1.74	0.76
Other	2.14	2.10
Total	100.00	100.00

Table 4-15
Company Drivers' Perceptions of Company Attitude toward Their
Welfare and Working Conditions,
Reported by Union Status and Age
(percent)

	Driver's Age		
	<25	25-50	>50
Union Drivers			
Very concerned	19.23	12.35	20.71
Reasonably concerned	30.77	34.67	38.69
Some concern	26.92	33.75	28.85
No concern	23.08	19.23	11.75
Total	100.00	100.00	100.00
Nonunion Drivers			
Very concerned	34.15	30.50	39.33
Reasonably concerned	30.48	34.00	31.46
Some concern	29.27	25.83	15.73
No concern	6.10	9.67	13.48
Total	100.00	100.00	100.00

Table 4-16
Seniority with Present Company,
Reported by Years of Driving Experience of Driver and Union Status
(percent)

Years of Driving Experience	Years Driving with Present Company or Driving for Self					
	0-2	3-5	6-10	11-25	>25	Total
Union Drivers						
0- 2	100.00	NA	NA	NA	NA	100.00
3- 5	51.23	48.77	NA	NA	NA	100.00
6-10	35.05	30.28	34.67	NA	NA	100.00
11-25	17.82	17.10	37.30	37.78	NA	100.00
>25	8.20	7.32	10.77	48.18	25.52	100.00
Nonunion Drivers						
0- 2	100.00	NA	NA	NA	NA	100.00
3- 5	54.67	45.33	NA	NA	NA	100.00
6-10	39.95	32.56	27.49	NA	NA	100.00
11-25	34.52	21.00	21.89	22.60	NA	100.00
>25	15.44	16.11	14.09	29.53	24.83	100.00

The general perception of the union company driver is that driving income provides an average or better than average standard of living. This perception is significantly higher than that of nonunion drivers. However, the union company driver perceives that his or her company is less concerned about the driver's welfare and work conditions. This relatively negative view of union employers' concern appears to be most closely related to cab work conditions and perceptions of equipment condition and is only moderately related to driving hours and dispatching practices.

These observations have important implications for the union and the organized employers. First, the union owner-operators clearly do not behave like the mainstream of the union membership. Second, the union company drivers are relatively satisfied with their economic situation, but are significantly more negative about their employers than their nonunion counterparts. As the drivers have become more secure financially, they are less willing to work long hours or cope with equipment that falls below their expectations. Wage settlements will have to be very large to buy off the union company driver's distress on these points. Can these points be dealt with in negotiations? Does this signal the dawning of an era of greater emphasis being put on work rule and other nonmonetary issues in contract negotiations? If the negotiations do turn in this direction, will the result be constraining work rules that further reduce management prerogative and hamper flexibility, countering one of the keys to the success of the truck in intermodal competition?

5 Attitudes about Equipment Condition

Professional truck drivers demonstrate strong feelings about the equipment they operate. These feelings resemble a love-hate relationship in which the driver has a sense of pride of the truck but also sees it as a symbol of resentment and personal threat.

This study focused on the drivers' perceptions of equipment condition rather than evaluating the relative merits of specific makes or models of trucks. The truck as a working environment is discussed in chapter 6.

I asked questions about tractors and trailers. The individual equipment systems evaluated included tires, electrical, engine (tractor only), and suspension.

Young and Old Drivers Are Different

Very young drivers (under age 25) were significantly less critical of their tractor condition. Older drivers tended to be slightly less critical of their tractors than the middle-aged group. (See table 5-1.) These observations appeared to reflect several attitudes. The younger drivers had lower expectations regarding equipment condition. Also, a significant proportion of younger drivers were owner-operators, who as a group tended to believe that their equipment was relatively safe. The older drivers' attitudes were explained by comments to the effect that "trucks are a lot safer now than they were in the past." These attitudes related to perceptions about truck condition rather than design.

Drivers showed great concern about the condition of tractor brakes, engines, and suspension. Comments were directed at the design and reliability of brake systems. Also, drivers strongly believe that trailer brakes are less safe than tractor brakes. It is difficult to interpret what constituted an unsafe engine in the drivers' perceptions. It might have been a reference to unreliable engines, but individual driver's comments lead me to believe that the drivers were really saying that they felt that tractors were potentially underpowered in emergency situations. The suspension system was the only equipment system that drivers felt was less safe on tractors than on trailers. While drivers may have been demonstrating concern about steering problems, a strong relationship between reports of "unsafe" tractor suspensions and vibration problems suggests that drivers were simply reacting to ride quality rather than to the truck's unsafe condition.

Table 5-1
Proportion of Drivers Who Consider Equipment Unsafe,
Reported by Age
(percent)

	Driver's Age		
Equipment System	<25	25-50	>50
Tractor			
Tires	2.7	5.7	4.4
Electrical	1.3	4.6	3.1
Brakes	5.0	13.7	11.2
Engine	3.7	10.7	7.1
Suspension	7.3	21.0	15.1
Trailer			
Tires	10.3	9.1	4.9
Electrical	13.3	7.3	4.7
Brakes	14.6	18.3	13.9
Suspension	9.3	8.3	5.8

Perceptions of Trailer Condition

Table 5-1 shows a pattern of driver responses that was found repeatedly in the study. Drivers generally believe that trailers are significantly less safe than tractors. This is partly explained by the ownership of trailers. Owner-operators are more critical of trailers owned by others. However, even after controlling for this situation, there is still evidence that drivers believe that trailers are less safe. Why? There is a general belief held by many drivers that less attention is paid to trailer maintenance. In fact, trailer maintenance is substantially easier than tractor maintenance. Tire wear on trailers is lighter, and most components requiring service are easily accessible. Perhaps the very ease of trailer maintenance makes it more casual, or gives the drivers the impression of casualness.

Of course, drivers are more likely to be assigned to a specific tractor, while this is a less typical practice with trailers. Drivers develop more of a sense of identity with a tractor and may be more insistent on maintaining it. Trailers are more typically seen as interchangeable equipment that is less frequently assigned to a specific driver.

Regardless of the reasons for the attitude, drivers do have different attitudes about the safety of different types of trailers, as seen in table 5-2. It is not directly apparent why drivers do believe that vans are the least safe trailers. It may be related to the fact that few vans are specifically dedicated to individual drivers, while other types of trailers are more likely to be either dedicated to or owned by a driver.

Table 5-2
Proportion of Company Drivers Who Consider Equipment Unsafe,
Reported by Type of Trailer
(percent)

| Type of Trailer | Equipment System | | | |
	Tires	Electrical	Brakes	Suspension
Van	6.2	4.5	15.6	11.5
Tank	4.1	1.5	9.6	3.3
Reefer	4.1	3.9	4.3	3.5
Flatbed	1.3	1.3	2.8	2.6
Moving van	1.4	1.9	3.3	1.4
Dump	1.0	1.0	1.0	3.0
Special	5.4	4.0	11.7	9.8

Another explanation of the drivers' sensitivity about trailer condition may stem from fear of the trailer. Many drivers see the trailer as a life-threatening object in the event of an accident. There is a fear of shifting cargo, jackknife, or other loss of control of the trailer. Drivers see the trailer as the most direct cause of serious injury to themselves in the event of an accident.

This offers a substantial opportunity for truck lines and manufacturers to take steps to deal with drivers' attitudes.

Equipment Safety and Employees' Attitudes toward Employers

Drivers' perceptions of equipment condition are closely associated with their attitudes about their employers. Table 5-3 reports the perceptions of company drivers about company attitude and condition of equipment. It is important to note that table 5-3 deals only with company drivers and specifically excludes owner-operators. There is a strong and consistent pattern that drivers who feel their equipment is unsafe also believe that their employer has little or no concern for them. This relationship may be explained in several ways. First, drivers who have negative attitudes about their employers may simply be more critical of equipment condition. Second, it may be that the belief that they are required to drive equipment thought unsafe leads drivers to the attitude that the company has less concern or interest in them. Third, both attitudes may simply be reflections of another issue—the quality of management that produces negative attitudes about equipment and concern for drivers. From a strict statistical viewpoint, it is difficult to determine a cause-and-effect relationship, if there is one. However, remarks made by drivers in the comment section of the question-

Table 5-3
Proportion of Company Drivers Who Consider Equipment Unsafe,
Reported by Driver's Perception of Company Attitude
(percent)

	Perception of Company Attitude			
Equipment System	Very Concerned	Reasonably Concerned	Some Concern	No Concern
Tractor				
Tires	1.4	2.4	8.4	17.4
Electrical	0.9	1.4	6.7	14.4
Brakes	2.6	6.8	20.3	42.4
Engine	2.3	4.5	16.4	29.4
Suspension	3.4	12.7	33.6	52.8
Trailor				
Tires	1.5	3.7	12.5	21.2
Electrical	1.7	2.5	9.8	17.2
Brakes	3.5	8.5	27.3	48.9
Suspension	1.7	3.2	11.3	24.7

naire leave no doubt in my mind about the interpretation of these observations. Equipment condition, or drivers' perceptions about equipment safety, is the single most important (non-income-related) factor influencing employee attitude.

If perception of equipment safety is such an important determinant of company attitude, it would be useful to focus attention on equipment systems to which drivers are most sensitive. Table 5-3 provides strong clues in this regard. Tractor suspensions and tractor and trailer brakes are clearly the areas of major contention. The implications for employers are clear. It is worth noting that the implications for the IBT and other driver organizations representing drivers' interests are significant. One might conclude that the best way to serve drivers beyond simple income interests involves leading the struggle to ensure equipment safety. However, another conclusion might be that one approach to organize a nonunion operator would be to attack the target company on the issue of equipment safety.

Perceptions of Owner-Operators Compared to Company Drivers

A long-standing debate has existed regarding the relative safety of equipment operated by owner-operators compared to company-owned equipment. Similarly, there have been debates about the comparative safety of equipment of exempt, private, and regulated segments of the industry.

Several issues must be considered in a discussion of these matters. First, what role does equipment condition play in accidents? Second, what constitutes "safe" equipment condition? Is there a minimum level of condition which is critical? For example, there appears to be a minimum tire-tread depth necessary for safe operation, but little increased safety is achieved by deeper tread. A minimum set of marker, brake, and directional lights seems necessary for safe operation. Are more lights safer? Third, what are the relative roles of "objective measures" and "subjective perceptions" of equipment condition and safety?

An argument can be made that few trucking accidents are caused by equipment failure. Table 5-4 strongly supports the position that the other causes are more critical. This is an interesting position that may appeal to the operator who is tempted to short-cut on equipment maintenance. However, there are strong arguments made by PROD that the Bureau of Motor Carrier Safety data in table 5-4 may be misleading. They are based primarily on reports of companies who have little incentive or inclination to point out that maintenance practices contributed to an accident. More detailed on-the-spot, independent investigations suggest that equipment condition or failure figures in more accidents than this table suggests. However, the argument about the level of accidents caused by equipment failure may not be as relevant as the simple fact that it is a significant cause that must not be ignored. It is clear that a driver's perceptions of safe equipment condition may not be directly related to objective measures

Table 5-4
Proportion of Reported Accidents Caused by Mechanical Failures, 1974-1975
(percent)

	Reportable Accidents		Reportable Fatalities		Reportable Injuries	
Cause of Accident	1974	1975	1974	1975	1974	1975
Mechanical failures	6.39	5.78	3.42	3.45	4.91	4.90
Other causes	93.61	94.22	96.58	96.55	95.09	95.10
Total	100.00	100.00	100.00	100.00	100.00	100.00

Source: Adapted from *Accidents of Motor Carriers of Property*, U.S. Department of Transportation, Bureau of Motor Carrier Safety, various years.

Table 5-5
Proportion of Drivers Who Consider Equipment Unsafe, Reported by Type of Operation and Regulatory Status
(percent)

Equipment System	Company Drivers				Owner-Operators			
	Exempt	*Private*	*Contract*	*Common*	*Exempt*	*Private*	*Contract*	*Common*
Tractor								
Tires	9.0	3.3	5.6	6.8	1.0	NA	0.3	1.1
Electrical	9.0	4.9	5.9	5.0	1.0	NA	0.5	0.4
Brakes	10.1	9.6	11.2	17.3	2.0	NA	0.3	2.7
Engine	5.6	5.6	9.6	12.8	4.0	NA	1.0	0.7
Suspension	11.2	11.7	11.7	27.2	2.0	NA	1.2	1.8
Trailer								
Tires	15.9	6.9	6.9	9.0	4.1	NA	6.6	5.3
Electrical	13.6	10.2	7.1	6.5	5.2	NA	7.7	5.3
Brakes	20.5	15.4	14.5	21.1	3.1	NA	8.3	6.2
Suspension	9.1	8.1	6.5	9.3	2.1	NA	4.4	2.7

of safety and safe condition. Some drivers may not have a sound basis of judging safety of equipment condition and may form impressions on irrelevant cues. For example, how much does the condition of paint or the addition of chrome accessories influence a driver's perception of equipment safety? Finally, how does the driver's perception of equipment influence driving behavior? Are drivers who are less confident of the condition of their brakes more likely to be more cautious?

With these notes of caution as a background, I turn to table 5–5. It is seen that, across the board, the owner-operators consider their equipment to be safer than company drivers do. Similarly, common-carrier company drivers do not feel their equipment is safer than other groups, a view that is contrary to that held by many truckline managers. Note which systems the common-carrier drivers are most critical of: tractor suspensions, tractor and trailer brakes, and engines. Common-carriers are more likely to specify less costly, harder-riding suspensions that may be perfectly adequate on safety grounds. Also, these carriers certainly do specify lower-horsepower engines. Judgment of the relative safety of each category should be suspended until the discussion of other safety practices, which is the subject of chapter 10.

Table 5–6
Proportion of Units Found with Defects When Inspected by the Bureau of Motor Carrier Safety in Roadside Checks, Reported by Equipment System and Regulatory Status, July 1971 through June, 1973
(percent)

Equipment System	Exempt	Private	Authorized[a]
Tractor			
Tires	5.9	4.7	5.7
Electrical	35.3	36.1	27.4
Brakes	61.4	52.6	67.4
Suspension	2.6	2.3	4.7
Steering	1.6	1.9	3.1
Trailer			
Tires	17.1	12.6	14.9
Electrical	41.9	55.7	49.1
Brakes	26.6	30.3	30.3
Suspension	8.4	7.1	7.9

Source: Adapted from *Safety Road Checks, Motor Carrier of Property*, U.S. Department of Transportation, Bureau of Motor-Carrier Safety, various years.

[a]Carriers performing operations under economic regulation of the Interstate Commerce Commission. This includes common and contract carriers.

Table 5-7
Proportion of Drivers Who Consider Equipment Unsafe,
Reported by Responsibility for Equipment Repair
(percent)

| | How Drivers Handle Safety Defects | | | | |
Equipment System	Personally Responsible	Always Report	Usually Report	Report If Bad	Don't Bother Reporting
Tractor					
Tires	1.5	.5.0	4.9	6.4	21.4
Electrical	1.4	3.7	3.1	6.4	17.2
Brakes	3.5	12.4	13.9	20.5	44.3
Engine	2.5	9.3	9.5	9.6	36.6
Suspension	4.3	19.4	22.6	21.8	57.6
Trailer					
Tires	3.5	7.0	8.9	14.1	29.5
Electrical	2.9	5.7	7.4	21.2	26.2
Brakes	5.4	15.8	19.4	31.4	56.3
Suspension	2.0	6.8	8.5	11.5	31.1

Owner-operators strongly believe that their equipment is safe. There is independent evidence that generally supports this view, although not as strongly as the owner-operators themselves might believe.

A comparison of drivers' perceptions in table 5-5 and the results of physical inspections summarized in table 5-6 is interesting. Unfortunately, the Bureau of Motor Carrier Safety (BMCS) inspections did not differentiate between owner-operators and company drivers. However, it is interesting to note that the BMCS roadside inspections showed more evidence of electrical and brake defects than the drivers thought they had. The two tables show similar results on tires, but the drivers were much more sensitive to tractor suspension problems than physical inspections of equipment showed. Of course, the driver may have more real dynamic information from riding in the tractor than the most careful static roadside examination could ever provide.

The differences in the actual and the perceived condition of equipment may be partly related to how the driver perceives her or his responsibility for the equipment condition. Table 5-7 examines this relationship. Drivers who are directly responsible for the condition of their equipment believe their tractors and trailers are safer. It may be that these drivers, because of personal involvement or sense of responsibility, have convinced themselves that their equipment is relatively safer. This may reflect a degree of unjustified overconfidence.

Summary

Truck drivers are very sensitive about the condition of their equipment, and there appears to be a strong association between employees' perception of equipment safety and of the company's attitude towards them. Perception of equipment safety does appear to be a determinant of attitude rather than the reverse.

Suspensions and brakes are the points of greatest concern to drivers. Engines are another concern. It is not clear that drivers are accurate or unbiased judges of truck conditions, and they may rely on inappropriate cues to determine equipment condition. Drivers who handle their own maintenance or feel responsible for their equipment believe their equipment is safer.

6

Work Conditions and How Drivers Cope with Them

Truck driving is a physically and emotionally demanding task. Truck drivers, in a sense, are quite isolated in their work environment although they are on the highway with other drivers and possibly operating with a codriver. The truck tractor is a piece of heavy industrial equipment powered by a large power plant. This chapter examines the reaction of drivers to this work environment and the practices of drivers attempting to cope with these conditions.

Work Conditions

I have divided the drivers' work conditions into three categories: cab conditions, on-the-road conditions, and personal conditions. Drivers' perceptions of these conditions differ substantially with age and several other characteristics of the driver.

Table 6-1 summarizes drivers' attitudes toward the environment of the tractor cab. The youngest drivers appeared to be less sensitive to all the environmental conditions studied. As recalled from chapter 5, drivers in this same age group are less critical of the condition of tractor safety as well. This may be because of lower expectations or lower levels of experience of this age group. There was some evidence of a spirit of machismo among these drivers. Perhaps they were even slightly embarrassed to complain too much about their trucks. As discussed in chapter 5, perhaps the older drivers' attitudes reflected a belief that the present conditions are greatly improved over what they had experienced in the past.

The seat receives great attention from most drivers. The major problem I did not expect was cleanliness. Since the maintenance of cab cleanliness is largely the task of the driver, it may seem ironic to truckline managers that so many drivers would identify this as a problem. Of course, this issue was more common among company drivers than among owner-operators.

In table 6-2 younger drivers tended to find monotony and boredom, loneliness, and most other on-the-road work conditions more of a problem. Since I found that younger drivers were more likely to have misrepresented log books or exceeded the 10-hour driving limit, it was expected that they would be more sensitive to federal and state inspections. What is something of a surprise is that the machismo spirit of young drivers that was reflected in their attitude toward cab work conditions does not extend to perceptions about road conditions, bad

Table 6-1
Cab Work Conditions,
Proportion of Drivers Who Find Each Feature to Be a Major Problem,
Reported by Age of Driver
(percent)

	Driver's Age		
Item	*<25*	*25-50*	*>50*
Noise	6.1	14.8	13.7
Vibration	9.1	18.0	14.1
Fumes	3.7	12.9	14.0
Seating	10.1	20.2	16.9
Temperature/humidity	6.8	17.5	15.2
Cleanliness	9.6	25.0	25.4

Table 6-2
On-the-Road Work Conditions,
Proportion of Drivers Who Find Each Feature to Be a Major Problem,
Reported by Age of Driver
(percent)

	Driver's Age		
Item	*<25*	*25-50*	*>50*
Monotony/boredom	9.5	7.3	6.0
Loneliness	12.8	7.2	3.5
Road conditions	27.0	25.3	18.2
Bad weather	21.6	17.6	17.1
Night driving	2.4	2.9	2.4
Other drivers	19.8	17.4	10.2
Federal and state inspections	31.9	12.1	6.3
Long driving hours	4.4	9.7	9.8
Responsibility for cargo	6.7	3.4	2.9
Loading and unloading	13.1	7.7	5.6
Unreasonable dispatches	16.2	17.0	14.9

Table 6–3
Personal Aspects of Work Conditions,
Proportion of Drivers Who Find Each Feature to Be a Major Problem,
Reported by Age of Driver
(percent)

| | Driver's Age | | |
Item	<25	25–50	>50
Separation from home	15.0	17.0	12.2
Lack of exercise	14.1	20.6	17.8
Irregular hours	11.7	24.1	23.3

weather, and other drivers. These features seem to bother young drivers while the older drivers appear to learn to cope with such problems. Or, perhaps a degree of self-selection has occurred so that drivers who were particularly bothered by these conditions have left the industry by this stage of life.

Table 6–3 suggests that the younger driver and older driver are slightly less sensitive to problems of separation from home, lack of exercise, and irregular hours. This may reflect fewer family attachments, a sense of machismo, and enjoyment of travel for the young driver. Again, the older drivers appear to be reflecting some element of self-selection or reconciliation with the lifestyle of the over-the-road driver.

In chapter 5 we found a strong association between drivers' perceptions of equipment condition and of the company's attitude toward the driver. The same relationship occurs in table 6–4. Just as drivers relate perceptions of equipment safety to company attitude, they react similarly to cab work conditions. There is slightly less evidence of this relationship in most items in tables 6–5 and 6–6. For example, most levels of complaint from the most positive to the most negative employees are only 1½ to 3 times as high. However, two categories stand out: long driving hours and unreasonable dispatches. Are these items which particularly contribute to negative attitude? Or, are these two items negative drivers are particularly sensitive to?

Dozing and Falling Asleep While Driving

The modern truck tractor has been designed to substantially reduce the requirements for physical strength of the driver. The problem facing the over-the-road truck driver today on the highway is how to remain alert. For this reason, I have focused my attention on the tendency of drivers to lose alertness, as evidenced in the extreme case of dozing or falling asleep at the wheel while driving. I fully

Table 6–4
Cab Work Conditions,
Proportion of Drivers Who Find Each Feature to Be a Major Problem,
Reported by Driver's Perception of Company Attitude
(percent)

	Perception of Company Attitude			
Item	Very Concerned	Reasonably Concerned	Some Concern	No Concern
Noise	5.0	10.9	21.8	32.1
Vibration	6.5	13.4	25.1	39.2
Fumes	8.5	9.9	19.2	30.9
Seating	8.4	15.8	28.5	44.1
Temperature/humidity	8.0	13.3	25.0	36.5
Cleanliness	13.6	19.4	39.7	51.0

Table 6–5
On-the-Road Work Conditions,
Proportion of Drivers Who Find Each Feature to Be a Major Problem,
Reported by Driver's Perception of Company Attitude
(percent)

	Perception of Company Attitude			
Item	Very Concerned	Reasonably Concerned	Some Concern	No Concern
Monotony/boredom	4.2	5.8	8.7	12.4
Loneliness	4.7	4.0	6.6	10.1
Road conditions	15.6	19.4	24.9	32.8
Bad weather	13.9	14.7	18.9	24.9
Night driving	2.1	2.1	3.4	5.0
Other drivers	13.1	13.0	15.8	19.6
Federal and state inspections	7.3	4.9	6.7	9.6
Long driving hours	3.2	5.3	13.7	25.7
Responsibility for cargo	1.7	1.4	3.1	5.5
Loading and unloading	3.8	3.2	5.3	8.6
Unreasonable dispatches	4.3	6.8	20.8	43.3

Table 6-6
Personal Aspects of Work Conditions,
Proportion of Drivers Who Find Each Feature to Be a Major Problem,
Reported by Driver's Perception of Company Attitude
(percent)

	Perception of Company Attitude			
Item	*Very Concerned*	*Reasonably Concerned*	*Some Concern*	*No Concern*
Separation from home	8.0	10.4	19.8	27.3
Lack of exercise	10.7	17.9	23.0	35.8
Irregular hours	9.7	18.7	35.5	52.0

recognize the potential danger of a driver operating at any diminished level of concentration. However, dozing or falling asleep while driving is the most dangerous level of this problem. As a practical matter, it is a condition that the drivers themselves can directly observe has occurred.

Not only is dozing or falling asleep at the wheel a major cause of accidents, as can be seen in table 6-7, but the types of accidents related to this physical condition, like drunkenness and sickness, are most likely to cause both high property damage and death to the driver and others who share the highway.

Which drivers are most likely to experience the problem of dozing, and how prevalent is it? Table 6-8 shows that the problem is not necessarily restricted to any regulatory status. It is definitely inversely related to age. Younger drivers are more likely to doze. Either older drivers have learned how to avoid dozing or those older drivers with a tendency to doze have left the industry, hopefully without an accident.

One would believe that regular compliance with the 10-hour driving limitation reduces the tendency to doze. This is supported in table 6-9. In fact, the proportion of drivers who report dozing is substantially higher among drivers who admit regularly exceeding the 10-hour limitation. Also, as seen in table 6-9, the proportion of drivers who never experience dozing is substantially higher among drivers who never exceed the 10-hour limit. The distressing point is that approximately two percent of the drivers in the study indicate that they have dozed once, twice, or more in the past year. Since one dozing incident could be fatal to the driver or others, this is a distressing finding.

Table 6-7
Severity of Truck Accidents,
Reported by Condition of Driver

Driver Condition at Time of Accident	Percentage of Accidents	Average Driver Fatalities per Accident	Average Driver Injuries per Accident	Reported Property Damage ($)
Dozing	1.8	0.063	0.537	13,884
Drunk	0.5	0.023	0.405	12,373
Sick	0.2	0.026	0.462	9,538
Other[a]	0.4	0.200[b]	0.305	11,575
Normal or no evidence	97.1	0.012	0.272	6,314
Total	100.0			

Source: Adapted from *Accidents of Motor Carriers of Property*, U.S. Department of Transportation, Bureau of Motor Carrier Safety, 1975, p. 61.

[a]Includes heart attack, blackout, and so on.

[b]Includes fatalities due to heart attack, and so on.

Impact of Fatigue

The 10-hour driving limit is not universally accepted as a suitable measure or limit of fatigue. Several organizations are actively promoting the lowering of the limit, while many drivers, in fact, exceed the limit daily. However, the 10-hour limitation is one benchmark that most drivers are aware of. I compared the perceptions of problems in the work environment of drivers who stated they seldom or never exceeded the 10-hour limitation with the perceptions of drivers who stated they regularly abused this law. I was looking to see what differences in tolerances, or intolerances, there were to particular problems. Table 6-10 suggests that drivers who showed greatest compliance with the 10-hour limitation were the most sensitive to problems associated with cab work conditions. Or, perhaps those drivers who were least sensitive to cab work conditions were more likely to exceed regularly the 10-hour driving limitation. Perhaps this sensitivity reduced their desire or willingness to exceed the 10-hour limit.

A different pattern emerges in table 6-11. Here we find a general increase in sensitivity to on-the-road conditions among drivers who regularly exceed the 10-hour limitation. One would expect increased sensitivity to monotony and boredom, loneliness, long driving hours, and unreasonable dispatches. Of course, exceeding the 10-hour driving limit does result in greater likelihood and increased severity of problems with federal and state inspections. The troublesome

Table 6–8
Experience of Drivers Dozing or Falling Asleep at Wheel While Driving,
Reported by Regulatory Status and Age of Driver
(percent)

Experience Dozing or Falling Asleep at Wheel	Regulatory Status				Driver's Age		
	Exempt	Private	Contract	Common	<25	25–50	>50
Never	28.86	26.11	36.93	31.84	26.76	29.35	43.61
Once or twice	37.81	46.96	38.50	38.18	42.14	40.28	33.40
Occasionally	31.34	25.51	23.00	28.19	28.76	28.49	22.00
Regularly	1.99	1.42	1.57	1.79	2.34	1.88	0.99
Total	100.00	100.00	100.00	100.00	100.00	100.00	100.00

Table 6-9
Experience of Dozing or Falling Asleep at Wheel,
Reported by Drivers Exceeding the 10-Hour Driving Limit
(percent)

	Frequency of Exceeding 10-Hour Driving Limit			
Experience of Dozing or Falling Alseep at Wheel	*Never*	*Once or Twice*	*Occasionally*	*Regularly*
Never	40.70	24.16	28.50	22.37
Once or twice	36.07	47.35	36.95	38.50
Occasionally	22.01	27.41	32.68	34.68
Regularly	1.22	1.08	1.87	4.27
Total	100.00	100.00	100.00	100.00

Table 6-10
Cab Work Conditions,
Proportion of Drivers Who Find Each Feature to Be a Major Problem,
Reported by Frequency the Driver Exceeds the 10-Hour Driving Limit
(percent)

	Frequency of Exceeding 10-Hour Driving Limit		
Item	*Never, Once or Twice*	*Occasionally*	*Regularly*
Noise	14.8	13.9	11.2
Vibration	16.9	17.1	14.3
Fumes	13.7	12.4	7.2
Seating	19.8	18.2	13.5
Temperature/humidity	16.8	15.7	13.8
Cleanliness	26.8	22.7	13.0

increases of intolerance to road conditions, bad weather, and other drivers raise serious quesions about the drivers' abilities to perform in a calm, patient, and safe manner, particularly in a demanding situation.

Table 6-12 reinforces what we observed in table 6-10. Drivers who exceed the 10-hour limitation are more likely to find separation to be a major problem. The need for exercise does not seem to be a problem that is increased. But drivers who work more hours are less likely to find irregular hours a problem. They may work more hours because they are not particularly sensitive to work-

Table 6-11
On-the-road Work Conditions,
Proportion of Drivers Who Find Each Feature to Be a Major Problem,
Reported by Frequency the Driver Exceeds the 10-Hour Driving Limit
(percent)

Item	Frequency of Exceeding 10-Hour Driving Limit		
	Never, Once or Twice	Occasionally	Regularly
Monotony/boredom	5.9	7.7	10.7
Loneliness	4.5	8.5	12.9
Road conditions	20.3	26.8	33.3
Bad weather	16.3	18.7	22.2
Night driving	2.7	2.4	2.3
Other drivers	13.3	15.6	25.3
Federal and state inspections	5.1	15.3	37.8
Long driving hours	7.7	11.9	14.6
Responsibility for cargo	2.2	4.4	7.8
Loading and unloading	3.3	10.2	24.5
Unreasonable dispatches	12.9	21.3	24.0

ing irregular hours. Or, perhaps they work so much of the time that the issue of *irregular* hours is irrelevant. If you work such long hours, there may be no irregular hours.

Methods of Staying Alert

There are many time-honored methods drivers use to stay alert. I asked drivers which they had tried and found effective. In retrospect, I discovered that this was a three-part question. First, had the driver tried the method? Second, if the driver had tried it, was the method effective? Third, was the driver presently using the method?

Table 6-13 unfortunately combines all three questions. I do not believe that this has a serious impact on the results except for the use of nonprescription stimulants and amphetamines, which some drivers might certainly hesitate to try.

The younger drivers are slightly less impressed with certain methods of staying alert, such as stopping, walking, washing the face, and driving with windows open, though these methods are still among the most popular mentioned by all groups. The younger drivers are more favorably impressed by using an AM or FM radio, singing or talking to themselves, and using the highly participative CB radio. It is interesting to note that the CB radio rates favorably with several

Table 6-12
Personal Aspects of Work Conditions,
Proportion of Drivers Who Find Each Feature to Be a Major Problem,
Reported by Frequency the Driver Exceeds the 10-Hour Driving Limit
(percent)

	Frequency of Exceeding 10-Hour Driving Limit		
Item	*Never, Once or Twice*	*Occasionally*	*Regularly*
Separation from home	13.2	18.6	22.2
Lack of exercise	19.3	20.3	17.2
Irregular hours	24.2	23.5	17.6

other methods of staying alert but has the advantage of allowing the driver to continue to drive and remain productive. Of course, this increased productivity is partly offset by an investment.

What have the "regular dozers" tried and found effective? As one would expect, in table 6-14 they find all methods less effective. But the use of the CB radio (while driving) or simply stopping and walking about is the most effective for this group.

How do drivers rest while on the road? Of course, many drivers operate in such a fashion that they do not have to rest. That is, they may return to their origin each day. It would be expected that this is more likely to occur with company drivers, particularly in the common, contract, and private industry segments. This is found to be the case in table 6-15.

The behavior of drivers who do find it necessary to rest is also reported in table 6-15. The sleeper cab is seen to be dominant among all types of exempt drivers and owner-operators operating for contract carriers. Use of hotels or motels is primarily found among company drivers outside the exempt area. The important finding in these data is the observation that such high proportions of company drivers "rest" in the seat of their tractor cabs. In table 6-16 we find that the tendency to doze is substantially higher for drivers who rest in this way. The only group of drivers who were more likely to doze were those who indicated "other" forms of rest, usually explained by the drivers as sleeping on the ground on the roadside.

Table 6–13
Proportion of Drivers Who Have Tried and Found Various
Methods of Staying Alert to Be Effective,
Reported by Age of Driver
(percent)

	Driver's Age		
Method	<25	25–50	>50
Stopping, walking, etc.	81.3	87.0	92.7
Washing face	63.3	74.5	78.8
Opening window	76.3	82.1	88.1
Listening to AM or FM radio	73.0	54.5	41.0
Using CB radio	86.3	86.7	75.4
Refreshment	85.3	87.5	89.7
Chewing gum or tobacco	40.0	41.0	37.7
Smoking	38.0	37.7	35.1
Singing or talking	72.3	65.4	62.5
Changing seat position	48.7	50.2	60.0
Nonprescription stimulant	18.7	11.6	4.6
Amphetamines	34.3	26.9	9.3

Table 6–14
Proportion of Drivers Who Have Tried and Found
Each Method of Staying Alert Effective,
Reported by Severity of Dozing Problem
(percent)

	Severity of Dozing Problem			
Method	Never	Once or Twice	Occasionally	Regularly
Stopping, walking, etc.	90.3	89.6	84.7	72.3
Washing face	75.7	77.5	72.7	60.0
Opening window	86.4	83.5	80.8	64.5
Listening to AM and FM radio	53.1	52.2	48.5	39.4
Using CB radio	80.8	85.7	84.9	74.8
Refreshment	91.2	87.9	85.5	69.7
Chewing gum or tobacco	41.7	40.0	38.6	30.3
Smoking	39.5	37.0	35.2	20.7
Singing or talking	35.9	65.9	66.9	51.6
Changing seat position	59.4	51.9	46.0	31.0
Nonprescription stimulant	6.4	10.5	13.1	18.7
Amphetamines	14.0	22.9	31.0	44.5

Table 6-15
How Drivers Rest While on the Road,
Reported by Type of Operation and Regulatory Status
(percent)

	Company Drivers				Owner-Operators			
	Exempt	*Private*	*Contract*	*Common*	*Exempt*	*Private*	*Contract*	*Common*
Do you rest on the road?								
Yes	3.80	7.00	12.30	25.07	7.95	NA	1.63	4.53
No	96.20	93.00	87.70	74.93	92.05	NA	98.37	95.47
Total	100.00	100.00	100.00	100.00	100.00	NA	100.00	100.00
If you do rest on the road, what method do you use?								
Sleeper cab	78.95	61.28	35.71	10.77	83.94	NA	90.95	86.10
Seat of cab	9.21	12.54	37.76	51.49	7.41	NA	3.88	5.69
Hotel or motel	5.26	23.40	23.72	31.74	6.17	NA	3.69	7.42
Rest station	1.32	0.84	1.28	2.87	1.24	NA	0.74	nil
Other	5.26	1.94	1.53	3.13	1.24	NA	0.74	0.79
Total	100.00	100.00	100.00	100.00	100.00	NA	100.00	100.00

Table 6-16
Experience of Dozing or Falling Asleep at Wheel,
Reported by Method Driver Uses to Rest While on the Road
(percent)

How Do You Rest on the Road?	Experience of Dozing or Falling Asleep While Driving				
	Never	*Once or Twice*	*Occasionally*	*Regularly*	*Total*
Don't rest	50.53	34.27	14.85	0.35	100.00
Sleeper cab	32.43	42.46	24.16	0.95	100.00
Seat of cab	17.23	38.35	40.97	3.45	100.00
Motel or hotel	38.19	37.63	23.17	1.01	100.00
Rest station	27.34	46.04	25.18	1.44	100.00
Other	39.34	33.88	24.59	2.19	100.00

Use of Drugs, Alcohol, and Other Substances to Cope with Working Conditions

There have been many reports of frequent use of various types of stimulants and pills to stay alert by drivers who abuse the 10-hour driving limitation. The use reported here was not as high as I had heard. Based on table 6-17, it is clear that there is heavier usage of pills among drivers who regularly exceed the 10-hour limitation. Of course, there are several segments of the industry where this abuse occurs most frequently. The "pep pills," it should be noted, are what drivers call bennies, goofballs, copilots, and so on. They are not the nonprescription stimulants. While I do not condone this level of use of such stimulants, it is much lower than the "folklore of the road" would suggest. That may not necessarily be good news. Perhaps there would be fewer accidents if drivers who insist on regularly exceeding the 10-hour limitation did use pep pills or other nonprescription stimulants. The question is, would encouragement to use such substances increase the abuse of the 10-hour limitation?

Table 6-18, when compared with table 6-19, shows a slightly higher level of abstention from alcoholic beverages among truck drivers of all types. But the willingness of drivers to operate their trucks immediately after or within one hour of drinking shows a high potential for drunk driving among some groups of drivers. This is particularly striking among the drivers under 25 years old (9.86 percent) and exempt drivers (10.45 percent).

The use of marijuana and narcotics while driving does occur. (See table 6-20.) Little research is available on the frequency of marijuana use by other types of workers at their place of work, so it is difficult to assess how the results of this survey compare to other groups of relatively indirectly supervised work-

Table 6-17
Use of Pep Pills,
Reported by Drivers Exceeding the 10-Hour Driving Limit
(percent)

	Frequency of Exceeding 10-Hour Driving Limit			
Use of Pep Pills	*Never*	*Once or Twice*	*Occasionally*	*Regularly*
Never	84.42	76.16	71.29	49.90
Once or twice	6.88	13.91	10.31	13.78
Occasionally	8.27	9.33	17.70	27.87
Regularly	0.43	0.60	0.70	8.45
Total	100.00	100.00	100.00	100.00

ers. As might be expected, the greatest use of marijuana reported was among the group of youngest drivers, which is consistent with the statistics for the population as a whole, as reported in table 6-21. The regular use of marijuana while driving is much lower than the levels of current use reported in table 6-21, but if one compares the proportion of drivers who use it (once or twice per year though regularly), it is found to be generally similar to the results for the total population figures.

The acceptability of the use of pep pills is an area of some dispute. Of course, as described here, we are dealing with serious substances, not nonprescription stimulants. The self-prescribed use of these substances can produce side effects that a driver might not expect. While drivers often find that they are more alert for some period after taking such a substance, repeated or continued use may lead to sudden complete lapse of consciousness or hallucinations. The 10.45 percent of the exempt drivers who use such pills regularly represent a great potential danger on the highway. Approximately 45 percent of the exempt drivers report that they regularly exceed the 10-hour driving limitation. It is difficult to assess which constitutes the greater hazard, but the driver who does both operates with an unrealistic sense of her or his alertness up to the point that loss of sense or control occurs.

Summary

Truck drivers are critical of the cab work conditions, with the youngest drivers showing the greatest tolerance. However, these same young drivers are generally less tolerant of the conditions they experience on the road.

Table 6-18
Attitude toward Alcoholic Beverages,
Reported by Regulatory Status and Age of Driver
(percent)

Attitude toward Alcoholic Beverages	Regulatory Status				Driver's Age		
	Exempt	*Private*	*Contract*	*Common*	*<25*	*25-50*	*>50*
Do not drink	50.74	49.18	47.49	47.22	47.28	45.07	56.75
Can drive satisfactorily without waiting	5.47	4.50	2.99	1.67	7.48	2.48	1.60
Wait about 1 hour to drive	4.98	2.25	0.88	0.80	2.38	1.13	0.68
Wait about 2 hours to drive	2.99	2.25	1.85	1.45	4.08	1.86	0.72
Wait about 3 hours to drive	1.99	0.82	1.76	0.90	2.38	1.15	0.60
Wait 4 hours or more to drive	33.83	40.98	45.03	47.96	36.40	48.31	39.65
Total	100.00	100.00	100.00	100.00	100.00	100.00	100.00

Table 6-19
Proportion of Population Age 18 and Over
Who Use Drugs and Alcohol, 1976

Type of Drug	Percent
Alcohol	58.8
Cigarettes	40.7
Cocaine	0.7
Heroin	a
Other Opiates	0.5

Source: Bureau of the Census, *Statistical Abstract of the U.S.*, 1977, table 182, p. 116.

aUnder 0.05 percent.

There is a strong association between the driver's attitude about the work environment of her or his cab and perception of the employer's attitude about drivers. Similar relationships appear to occur with the perceptions of number of hours driven and reasonableness of dispatches.

Dozing or falling asleep at the wheel, a frequent cause of major life-threatening accidents, was found to be more likely among the youngest drivers. Drivers who adhere to the 10-hour driving limitation show a much lower tendency to doze.

Drivers who exceed the 10-hour limitation reported that they were more sensitive to road and weather conditions and other drivers.

Stopping and walking about, a time-honored method of staying alert, is still ranked highly by drivers. The most effective means of staying alert without stopping are driving with an open window (at no captial investment) and use of the CB radio.

The majority of drivers who rest on the road use the bunk of a sleeper cab. However, a striking number of drivers say they "rest" in the seat of their cab, a method that is shown to have poor results in preventing dozing.

Truck drivers report use of alcoholic beverages at a level lower than the U.S. population over age 18 years. Compared to other truck drivers, there is a willingness of the youngest drivers and exempt and private carrier drivers to drive their trucks without waiting after drinking alcoholic beverages.

The use of marijuana generally appears to be at levels that are similar to those in the population overall. However, these drivers are stating that they are using this substance while driving, which may subject other drivers to danger.

Finally, the regular use of pep pills was not reported to be as great as the folklore of the highway would lead one to believe. However, it is particularly frequent among the exempt drivers. This, coupled with the high frequency of abuse of the 10-hour driving limitation, is a particularly dangerous combination for the drivers themselves as well as for other users of the highway.

Table 6-20
Use of Stimulants and Drugs While Driving
Reported by Regulatory Status and Age of Driver,
(percent)

Use of Stimulants and Drugs	Regulatory Status				Driver's Age		
	Exempt	Private	Contract	Common	<25	25-50	>50
Use of Narcotics While Driving							
Never	91.06	94.97	97.22	97.91	99.63	97.11	98.87
Once or twice	29.98	2.01	1.22	1.41	0.37	1.57	0.78
Occasionally	2.98	2.42	1.30	0.52	0.00	0.96	0.31
Regularly	2.98	0.60	0.26	0.16	0.00	0.36	0.04
Total	100.00	100.00	100.00	100.00	100.00	100.00	100.00
Use of Marijuana While Driving							
Never	86.14	91.11	92.70	97.17	77.41	95.12	99.17
Once or twice	6.93	3.84	3.48	1.59	8.97	2.57	0.67
Occasionally	3.96	3.23	2.70	0.85	9.30	1.59	0.16
Regularly	2.97	1.82	1.12	0.38	4.32	0.72	0.00
Total	100.00	100.00	100.00	100.00	100.00	100.00	100.00
Use of Pep Pills While Driving							
Never	48.26	68.89	74.61	86.55	61.28	71.71	90.08
Once or twice	11.94	10.51	10.47	10.60	13.80	11.31	4.64
Occasionally	29.35	18.18	13.87	2.65	20.20	15.40	5.00
Regularly	10.45	2.42	1.05	0.20	4.72	1.58	0.28
Total	100.00	100.00	100.00	100.00	100.00	100.00	100.00

Table 6-21
Proportion of Population Who Have Used or
Currently Use Marijuana, 1975-1976

Age	Percentage Ever Used	Percentage Currently Use
18–25	53	25
26–34	36	11
≥35	6	1

Source: *Bureau of the Census, Statistical Abstract of the U.S.*, table 183, 1977, p. 116.

7   Hazardous Materials

Tremendous quantities of hazardous materials move on the American highways. The handling of hazardous materials is of special concern to all who use the road because of the greater severity of accidents involving these commodites. As seen in table 7-1, the intensity of such accidents is higher.

Of course, not every commodity that is termed *hazardous material* is equally dangerous to the driver, other drivers, or bystanders. Also, proportion of hazardous loads carried by an individual driver may vary. Of the 9,630 drivers in the survey, 16 percent stated that they carried hazardous materials "regularly" while 50 percent indicated that they carried such materials "sometimes." Approximately 32 percent indicated they "seldom or never carried" hazardous materials, and 2 percent did not specify the extent to which they carried these materials.

I have compared the driving practices and attitudes of drivers who frequently carry hazardous materials with drivers who do so infrequently or seldom or never do so. While these terms are rather imprecise, these categories were useful. In fact, I have focused attention on the first and last categories for the purpose of comparison.

Safety Practice

One would hope that the drivers who most frequently carry hazardous materials would be among those who are most likely to comply with safety regulations. These would likely be the drivers with best driving records equipment, safety practices, and health.

Table 7-2 suggests that the drivers who frequently or sometimes carry hazardous materials drive at slightly lower average cruising speeds than other drivers do. They have substantially better experience on moving violations and adherence to the 10-hour driving limit. Of course, these are all positive signs.

Based on table 7-3, it appears that drivers who frequently carry hazardous materials are less likely to drive while intoxicated (95.89 percent do not drink or wait at least 4 hours to drive after drinking compared to 91.02 percent for other drivers). In fact, the proportion of frequent hazardous-materials drivers who drive without waiting after taking alcoholic beverages is appoximately half as great as the drivers who seldom or never carry such commodities.

Table 7-1
Accident Intensity, Comparing Damage Incurred in Accidents[a]
Reported to the U.S. Department of Transportation
Involving Hazardous Materials, 1975

Accident Intensity	Accidents Not Involving Hazardous Materials	Accidents Involving Hazardous Materials
Fatalities per accident	0.091	0.113
Injuries per accident	1.083	1.161
Property damage per accident	$6,366	$9,545

Source: Derived from U.S. Department of Transportation, Bureau of Motor-Carrier Safety, *1975 Accidents of Motor-Carrier of Property*.

[a]An *accident* is defined here as an event resulting in (1) the death of a human being, (2) bodily injury to a person who, as a result, receives medical treatment away from the scene of the accident, or (3) total damage to all property aggregating $2,000 or more.

Table 7-2
Driving Practices and Records of
Drivers Carrying Hazardous Materials

Item	Carry Hazardous Materials		
	Frequently	Sometimes	Seldom or Never
Cruising speed, mph	59.3	58.9	60.3
Moving violations per 100,000 miles	0.5	0.5	0.8
Regularly exceed 10-hour driving limit, percent	4.2	4.2	22.6

The same positive signs are generally seen in table 7-4. There is little difference between the drivers on the use of narcotics or marijuana. And there is definitely less use of pep pills among the drivers who carry hazardous materials. This might follow what would be expected from a group of drivers who seldom exceed the 10-hour driving limit.

However, adherence ot the 10-hour driving limit and avoidance of the use of pep pills are really potential measures of the probability of the driver being alert. How alert are the drivers who carry hazardous materials? In fact, according to the data in table 7-5, they may be less alert than other drivers. Of the drivers

Table 7-3
Attitude toward Alcoholic Beverages,
Reported by Drivers Carrying Hazardous Materials
(percent)

	Carry Hazardous Materials		
Attitude toward *Alcoholic Beverages*	*Frequently*	*Sometimes*	*Seldom* *or Never*
Do not drink	45.69	47.43	50.62
Can drive satisfactorily without waiting	1.70	1.51	3.98
Wait about 1 hour to drive	0.78	0.74	1.70
Wait about 2 hours to drive	0.85	1.55	2.12
Wait about 3 hours to drive	0.78	1.02	1.18
Wait 4 or more hours to drive	50.20	47.75	40.40
Total	100.00	100.00	100.00

in the sample who regularly carry hazardous materials, 1.8 percent report that they regularly "experience dozing or falling asleep at the wheel," a figure that is over twice as great as that of the drivers who seldom or never carry these commodities. Table 7-6 indicates that the drivers who carry hazardous materials do tend to be older. However, as discussed in chapter 6, the tendency to doze or fall alseep at the wheel is *generally* not correlated with the age of the driver.

Physical Condition

Turning to the physical condition of the drivers of hazardous materials, one might conclude from table 7-7 that these drivers may be in poorer physical condition than other drivers. In fact, even considering the variation in physical condition of drivers explained by the drivers' age (reported in table 2-7) and the relative seniority of these hazardous-materials drivers, one is still struck by the substantially higher-than-expected incidence of ulcers, nervousness, and frequent headaches, all symptoms of stress, which may also be the cause of fatigue leading to dozing.

Equipment Condition

If stress is a concern, one would expect drivers who carry hazardous materials to have more complaints about working hours. This is found to be true. Nearly 15 percent of the drivers who frequently carry hazardous materials complain about

Table 7-4
Use of Stimulants and Drugs,
Reported by Drivers Carrying Hazardous Materials
(percent)

	Carry Hazardous Materials		
Use of Stimulants and Drugs	*Frequently*	*Sometimes*	*Seldom or Never*
Use of Narcotics While Driving			
Never	98.55	97.76	96.84
Once or twice	0.13	1.25	1.69
Occasionally	0.86	0.79	1.09
Regularly	0.46	0.19	0.38
Total	100.00	100.00	100.00
Use of Marijuana While Driving			
Never	97.01	97.15	92.67
Once or twice	1.43	1.57	3.71
Occasionally	0.78	0.94	2.53
Regularly	0.78	0.33	1.09
Total	100.00	100.00	100.00
Use of Pep Pills While Driving			
Never	78.11	77.47	73.52
Once or twice	8.21	9.23	10.08
Occasionally	12.64	12.19	13.70
Regularly	1.04	1.11	1.80
Total	100.00	100.00	100.00

Table 7-5
Experience of Drivers Dozing or Falling Asleep at Wheel While Driving,
Reported by Drivers Carrying Hazardous Materials
(percent)

	Carry Hazardous Materials		
Experience of Dozing or Falling Asleep at Wheel	*Frequently*	*Sometimes*	*Seldom or Never*
Never	29.55	32.18	35.76
Once or twice	36.73	38.37	39.90
Occasionally	30.92	27.79	23.22
Regularly	2.80	1.65	1.12
Total	100.00	100.00	100.00

Table 7–6
Age Distribution of Drivers Carrying Hazardous Materials
(percent)

Age of Driver	Carry Hazardous Materials		
	Frequently	*Sometimes*	*Seldom or Never*
<25	1.17	1.04	7.41
25–50	68.83	69.16	71.97
>50	30.00	29.80	20.62
Total	100.00	100.00	100.00

Table 7–7
Drivers' Health Problems,
Reported by Frequency of Carrying Hazardous Materials
(percent)

Health Problem	Carry Hazardous Materials		
	Frequently	*Sometimes*	*Seldom or Never*
Visual	11.4	11.5	12.2
Hearing	10.4	8.2	5.7
Hernia	2.9	2.3	1.8
Back	27.2	21.9	16.3
Hemorrhoids	23.7	18.5	14.4
Ulcers	13.3	10.4	7.5
Diabetes	1.7	1.3	0.9
Kidney	5.9	4.4	2.9
High blood pressure	9.8	7.4	6.1
Low blood pressure	0.9	0.9	1.3
Heart	1.6	2.0	1.1
Nervous	10.7	6.8	3.5
Varicose veins	2.7	2.0	1.9
Frequent headaches	9.3	7.5	5.7

long driving hours compared with approximately 6 percent among the drivers who seldom or never carry such materials. This is even more striking a comparison when table 7-2 points out that the hazardous materials drivers drive fewer hours.

Based on table 7-8, it appears that company drivers who carry hazardous materials have perceptions of slightly higher standards of living. However, the greatest difference is seen among those drivers who seldom or never carry hazardous materials and all other drivers. I do not believe that drivers who frequently carry such materials believe their incomes are particularly higher, so I wonder if the stress is really rewarded.

What is the attitude of drivers who carry hazardous materials regarding the safety and condition of their equipment? Here we find rather startling results. As can be seen in table 7-9, the hazardous-materials drivers consider their equipment less safe than other drivers do. Of course, we are dealing with drivers' perceptions and expectations. The term *unsafe* is not precise and is very subjective. It might well be expected that hazardous-materials drivers are substantially more critical of their equipment condition than other drivers are. Their expectations of maintenance are likely to be higher. However, we may also be experiencing the situation that company drivers, which most hazardous-materials drivers are, generally reported their equipment to be in less safe condition than was reported by owner-operators. It is clear that hazardous-materials drivers do believe that their trailer systems are less safe than their truck systems.

The distressing point is that such a high proportion of the drivers who carry hazardous materials on the highways *believe* their equipment to be unsafe. Perhaps objective measures could be introduced that might show this equipment to be substantially the same as that used for nonhazardous materials. However, what we are dealing with here are the perceptions of the people who operate this equipment. And their perceptions are important for two reasons. First, these drivers are the closest to the situation. Second, they are under the emotional stress of believing that they are operating unsafe equipment, which may place them and others in jeopardy.

Table 7-8
Perceptions of Standard of Living of Company Drivers,
Reported by Drivers Carrying Hazardous Materials
(percent)

Perception of Standard of Living	Carry Hazardous Materials		
	Frequently	*Sometimes*	*Seldom or Never*
High	6.07	5.49	5.29
Above average	31.17	31.63	27.15
Average	59.90	60.82	59.28
Below average	2.86	2.06	8.28
Total	100.00	100.00	100.00

Table 7-9
**Proportion of Drivers Who Consider Their Equipment Unsafe,
Reported by Drivers Carrying Hazardous Materials**
(percent)

Equipment System	Carry Hazardous Materials		
	Frequently	*Sometimes*	*Seldom or Never*
Tractor			
Tires	8.6	6.4	1.9
Electrical	6.7	4.6	2.1
Brakes	20.8	15.7	4.6
Trailer			
Tires	12.4	8.4	5.8
Electrical	8.7	6.1	7.3
Brakes	24.7	19.9	9.5

Summary

In conclusion, it appears that hazardous-materials drivers generally demonstrate better driving records and more closely adhere to driving safe regulations pertaining to hours of service and the use of drugs and alcohol. The hazardous-materials drivers are older and presumably have more driving experince.

However, these drivers have a greater tendency to doze or fall asleep at the wheel, a dangerous situation, particularly for hazardous-material drivers. The hazardous-materials drivers show greater symptoms of stress than other drivers do. This is not explained by the seniority of these drivers.

Finally, a remarkably high proportion of hazardous-materials drivers believe their basic safety equipment systems are unsafe. Brake systems, obviously vital, are the worst offenders, with 20.8 and 24.7 percent of the drivers considering their tractor and trailer brakes (respectively) to be unsafe. This may be a matter of high expectations or supersensitivity on the part of these drivers. However, if the drivers are concerned, the other drivers on the highway might well be advised to be concerned as well.

8 Women Drivers

Little is known about the attitudes of women who are professional heavy-duty truck drivers. Of the 9,630 drivers included in the data base of this study, only 57 were women. Under most circumstances I would hesitate to report the results of such a small sample. However, this unusual minority in an industry that has been so strongly identified as male deserves special attention. Certainly this small sample of women should not necessarily be considered as typical women and their attitudes probably do not suggest what attitudes would be held by a larger population of women if they were to enter the industry. I caution the reader to take the data reported here as those of a small group of highly unusual individuals.

Demographics

Are women drivers more likely to be unmarried than their male counterparts? The survey shows that 40 percent of the women of the sample were unmarried, while only 11 percent of the men were unmarried. It should be noted that several of the women drivers drove with their husbands, but most did not. This is similar to other reports on this point.[1]

Women drivers in the sample were not as likely to be members of a union, as seen in table 8-1. This is probably partly explained by the types of commodities that they carried and the higher proportion of women working as owner-operators. As noted in table 8-2, there were high proportions of women in the sample carrying refrigerated products and general commodities, commodities that had 17.12 and 62.66 percent, respectively, union penetration among owner-operators in general. Articles about women drivers note their concentration in household goods carriage.[2] While it is a commodity group that women drivers participate in, it is significant to note that its importance may be overstated.

Perceptions of Standard of Living and Company Attitude

How do these women truck drivers see their income, companies, and working conditions? While the proportion of women who believe that their standard of living is high is greater than their male counterparts , so is the proportion who believe their standard of living was below average, as seen in table 8-3. The

Table 8-1
Union Status and Type of Operation,
Reported by Sex of Driver
(percent)

	Sex of Driver	
	Male	*Female*
Union Status		
Union	81.9	31.6
Nonunion	18.1	68.4
Total	100.0	100.0
Type of Operation		
Company drivers	79.2	54.7
Owner-operators	20.8	45.3
Total	100.0	100.0

Table 8-2
Proportion of Workforce that Reported Regularly
Carrying Each Commodity,
Reported by Sex of Driver
(percent)

Commodities Regularly Carried This Past Year	Sex of Driver	
	Male	*Female*
Iron and steel	11.76	5.26
Heavy metal objects, machinery	8.87	8.77
Motor vehicles	5.26	1.75
Bulk products	4.09	3.51
Farm products (not refrig.)	4.20	5.26
Refrigerated	7.44	40.35
General commodities	59.75	36.84
Livestock	0.51	5.26
Household goods	15.17	17.54
Building materials	15.43	14.04
Other	20.38	22.81

Table 8–3
Perceptions of Standard of Living,
Reported by Sex of Driver
(percent)

Perception of Standard of Living	Sex of Driver	
	Male	Female
High	5.0	7.3
Above average	27.4	14.6
Average	59.7	54.5
Below average	7.9	23.6
Total	100.0	100.0

sample size was too small to support finer cross tabulation. However, there was stronger representation of refrigerated-commodities drivers among the women who reported high standards of living. If these women are removed from the sample, the women appear to be much less satisfied regarding their incomes than the male drivers in the survey. This raises a question: Why have they not turned more to the union for wage gains?

Perhaps this question is partly explained by table 8–4. The women company drivers in the sample had considerably more positive attitudes toward their companies than the men did. Their attitude as a group was quite similar to the perceptions of all nonunion company drivers. Comments added to the question-naires of the women drivers suggested that their companies did have strong con-cerns for them and their success as drivers. Will this attitude of companies continue if women become more commonplace as professional drivers? Or, is this attitude simply a result of the notoriety that the rare women truck driver on the company's rolls might receive?

Turning to driving performance, several interesting observations are noted in table 8–5. First, women reported slightly faster driving speeds than the men. This may partly account for the higher incidence of moving violations that the women reported. However, the high rate of moving violations, over three times that of male drivers, was claimed by some women to be the result of sex bias of law enforcement officials. I have no way to test this claim. While there is lower incidence of dozing while driving, as listed in table 8–6, the data in table 8–7 shows higher regular use of pep pills and greater tendency to drive while under the influence of alcohol. What is of interest is the substantially lower level of "reportable accidents" reported by the women drivers.

How do women view their work conditions? Truck driving is generally thought of as being a physically demanding occupation. How do women stand

Table 8–4
Perceptions of Company Attitude Held by Company Drivers,
Reported by Sex of Driver
(percent)

	Sex of Driver	
Perception of *Company Attitude*	*Male*	*Female*
Very concerned	16.8	25.9
Reasonably concerned	35.5	44.5
Some interest	31.5	14.8
No concern	16.2	14.8
Total	100.0	100.0

Table 8–5
Driving Performance,
Reported by Sex of Driver

	Sex of Driver	
Item	*Male*	*Female*
Average speed, mph	59.4	61.1
Reportable Accidents per 100,000 miles	0.2	0.1
Moving violations per 100,000 miles	0.6	1.9

Table 8–6
Experience of Dozing or Falling Asleep at Wheel,
Reported by Sex of Driver
(percent)

	Sex of Driver	
Experience of Dozing or Falling *Asleep While Driving*	*Male*	*Female*
Never	33.0	45.6
Once or twice	38.5	28.0
Occasionally	26.8	24.6
Regularly	1.7	1.8
Total	100.0	100.0

Table 8-7
Use of Pep Pills and Alcohol,
Reported by Sex of Driver
(percent)

	Sex of Driver	
	Male	*Female*
Use of Pep Pills While Driving		
Never	76.3	77.2
Once or twice	9.6	7.1
Occasionally	12.8	12.2
Regularly	1.3	3.5
Total	100.0	100.0
Use of Alcohol While Driving		
Don't drink	48.2	55.4
Can drive satisfactorily without waiting	2.4	8.9
Wait about 1 hour to drive	1.1	Nil
Wait about 2 hours to drive	1.6	1.8
Wait about 3 hours to drive	1.0	1.8
Wait 4 hours or more to drive	45.7	32.1
Total	100.0	100.0

up to these demands? Based on table 8-8, the women in this sample appear to have fewer complaints about cab work conditions than the men do. This has been supported by remarks of women in interviews reported in the press.[3]

There may be several explanations of these different perceptions about cab work conditions. First, the women may feel that they have to put up a "brave face" on these items. To admit that they are bothered by cab work conditions might be too threatening. Second, the women may simply be more tolerant and forebearing of work conditions than the men. This greater tolerance of aggravation by women is often cited as the reason why women dominate the ranks of telephone operators. Finally, the women may have been assigned better equipment than the men. Probably all three explanations are partly correct. The data did show that the women were driving slightly newer trucks than the men in the sample. Table 8-9 suggests that women are certainly not timid about complaining about other work conditions. Most notably, significantly higher complaints were raised about bad weather, road conditions, night driving, and other drivers. Women drivers had more complaints of loading and unloading as a problem. The higher level of complaints by women about federal and state inspections raises some questions. There was no evidence of higher incidence of hours of service or log book rules. The slightly higher average cruising speed, use of pep pills, and willingness to drink and drive might contribute to this

Table 8-8
Cab Work Conditions, Proportion of Drivers Who Find
Each Feature to Be a Major Problem,
Reported by Sex of Driver
(percent)

	Sex of Driver	
Item	*Male*	*Female*
Noise	14.1	10.7
Vibration	16.7	12.3
Fumes	12.9	5.6
Seating	19.1	9.1
Temperature/humidity	16.6	13.0
Cleanliness	24.7	9.1

Table 8-9
On-the-Road Work Conditions, Proportion of Drivers
Who Find Each Feature to Be a Major Problem,
Reported by Sex of Driver
(percent)

	Sex of Driver	
Item	*Male*	*Female*
Monotony/boredom	7.0	9.1
Loneliness	6.5	4.6
Road Conditions	23.5	29.9
Bad weather	17.6	28.6
Night driving	2.7	12.5
Other drivers	15.2	19.6
Federal and state inspections	11.0	21.8
Long driving hours	9.6	8.8
Responsibility for cargo	3.3	7.3
Loading and unloading	7.2	17.5
Unreasonable dispatches	16.2	17.9

greater sensitivity about inspections. However, as stated earlier, this may also be a reflection of an attitude of enforcement officers.

In table 8-10, aside from greater complaints about a lack of exercise, the women in the sample found the personal aspects of their work conditions not appreciably more or less of a problem than the men did.

Table 8-10
Personal Aspects of Work Conditions, Proportion of Drivers
Who Find Each Feature to Be a Major Problem,
Reported by Sex of Driver
(percent)

	Sex of Driver	
Item	*Male*	*Female*
Separation from home	17.8	16.7
Lack of exercise	19.6	26.8
Irregular hours	20.6	19.3

Summary

It is difficult to draw any statistically valid conclusions based on a limited sample of presumably very unusual and highly visible women in a predominantly male workforce. However, the women in the sample appear to have more positive attitudes about their companies, though compared to the attitudes of men drivers, they are not as enthusiastic about their standard of living derived from their driving income. The women have fewer complaints about the cab work conditions, but this may be because of the equipment they are assigned. Their complaints about on-the-road work conditions are as high as or higher than the men. They have no greater complaints about loneliness, irregular hours, or separation than the men do, but then a greater proportion of the women are not married and may have substantially different family situations.

Finally, there seems to be a tendency for law enforcement officials to give women truck drivers more attention. The complaint of sex bias seems to be quite possibly true, but it seems to be working in favor as well as against the women in this sample.

Notes

1. "Move Over Male Chauvinists!" *Heavy Duty Trucking*, May 1973, pp. 28–39.
2. Ibid.
3. Ibid.

9 Owner-Operators

Owner-operator truckers are one of the most controversial groups of truck drivers in the United States. For many years these independent truckers were ignored by government policy makers, industry observers, and many people in the trucking industry itself. Because of the rapid growth of irregular-route truckload traffic, the national rebellion during the energy crisis in the winter of 1973 to 1974, and the organizing efforts of a few dedicated and vocal spokesmen, including Mike Parkhurst of *Overdrive* and Bill Hill of *FASH*, the owner-operator has become a more visible feature of the trucking industry. Recognition of the owner-operator by Congress and the Interstate Commerce Commission led to a series of hearings conducted throughout the United States with the purpose of learning more about the practices and financial conditions of these independent truckers.[1] These hearings produced great volumes of material, but most of it was situational and did not lend itself to statistical analysis. The following provides that statistical examination of this highly productive and unique workforce.

Equipment Ownership and Type of Operation

There are several ways to categorize owner-operators. First, owner-operators, as the term implies, operate equipment they own. However, while the owner-operator owns a tractor, this does not necessarily imply ownership of a trailer. In fact, in my survey, just under 40 percent of the owner-operators did operate their own trailer.

Second, owner-operators may be categorized by primary type of operation: (1) drive for self (truly independent), (2) trip lease, and (3) long-term lease. Of course, owner-operators quite often operate some mixture of these categories. An independent operator under long-term lease to one carrier may take a trip lease to another carrier for a return load. The owner-operators identified their *primary mode* of operation as follows: 33 percent drive for self, 17 percent trip lease, and 50 percent long-term lease, but it is understood that some switching between modes of operation does occur.

The drivers who drive for themselves have a slightly higher perception of their standard of living, as seen in table 9-1. They arrange for loads for themselves or use the services of a broker. While many rely on a company, they are more independent of this source than the trip or long-term leasors. It is seen in

85

Table 9-1
Perceptions of Standard of Living,
Reported by Type of Owner-Operator
(percent)

	Type of Owner-Operator		
Perception of *Standard of Living*	*Drive for* *Self*	*Trip* *Lease*	*Long-Term* *Lease*
High	3.90	2.81	2.86
Above average	19.48	15.00	13.45
Average	56.82	55.94	59.11
Below average	19.80	26.25	24.58
Total	100.00	100.00	100.00

table 9-2 that long-term leasors primarily depend on the company for this function. Only 9.62 percent find their own backhauls. Combining the results of tables 9-1 and 9-3 provides interesting comparisons. Most owner-operators feel "fine" about their situation. But the long-term leasors are least satisfied. The proportion who want out is well below the proportion who believe they made a below average standard of living, but the proportion who feel so satisfied about their situation is much larger than the proportion who believe they make an above average or higher standard of living.

Third, and perhaps one of the most interesting categorizations, is along the lines of what commodity the driver frequently carries. The survey was not an attempt to determine specifically the number of owner-operators or which commodities they carry. However, it was possible to study the combinations of commodities that owner-operators in the survey carried. For example, what other commodities are carried by owner-operators who regularly carried iron and steel? To examine this movement of owner-operators between commodities, table 9-4 was constructed. For example, of the owner-operators who stated that they regularly carried iron and steel this past year, 39.94 percent also regularly carried heavy metal and machinery and 40.45 percent also carried building materials. Table 9-4 provides this information for each major commodity group. It is interesting to observe the areas of greatest mobility of owner-operators among commodities. The iron and steel, heavy machinery, and building materials combinations appear to be a reasonable combination because the type of trailer used, shippers, and consignees are often the same. Some general commodities lend themselves to the same type of equipment. Similarly, there is some cross-over among general commodities, farm products (not refrigerated), and refrigerated products because of the van trailers used. One would expect that the tractor and household goods van would be so specialized that it would not be very suit-

Table 9–2
Owner-Operator Arrangements for Backhauls,
Reported by Type of Owner-Operator
(percent)

Typically Who Arranges Your Backhauls?	Type of Owner-Operator		
	Drive for Self	Trip Lease	Long-Term Lease
Broker	10.93	8.16	2.61
Self	34.62	16.31	9.62
Agent	4.25	5.67	3.33
Company	44.33	67.38	83.49
Other	5.87	2.47	0.95
Total	100.00	100.00	100.00

Table 9–3
Attitudes toward Continuing as an Owner-Operator,
Reported by Type of Owner-Operator
(percent)

	Type of Owner-Operator		
	Drive for Self	Trip Lease	Long-Term Lease
Attitude toward Being an Owner-Operator			
Fine	75.21	69.81	63.74
Want to continue but will not replace current equipment	14.48	14.78	21.28
Want out	10.31	15.41	14.98
Total	100.00	100.00	100.00

able for other commodities. This seems generally true except for some crossover to general commodities and building materials.

It is worth observing that there is some degree of mobility in nearly every commodity group, and this is one of the frequently observed aspects of owner-operator behavior. This switching appears to be inherent to their sense of independence, but may also provide opportunities to employ equipment for backhauls or in slack periods.

Table 9-4
Commodities Regularly Carried by Owner-Operators
(percent)

Other Commodities Regularly Carried This Past Year	Commodity Regularly Carried This Past Year							
	Iron and Steel	Heavy Metal, Machinery	Motor Vehicles	Farm Products	Refrigerated	General Commodities	Household Goods	Building Materials
Iron and steel	100.00	67.37	15.69	15.63	3.13	8.74	1.69	35.08
Heavy metal, machinery	39.94	100.00	25.49	13.54	2.68	8.20	4.52	20.92
Motor vehicles	2.01	5.51	100.00	1.04	0.45	0.36	1.98	1.31
Farm products (not refrig.)	3.77	5.51	1.96	100.00	9.38	4.74	1.69	5.88
Refrigerated	1.76	2.54	1.96	21.88	100.00	13.48	3.11	2.83
General commodities	12.06	19.07	3.92	27.08	33.04	100.00	31.36	21.79
Household goods	1.51	6.78	13.73	6.25	4.91	20.22	100.00	8.93
Building materials	40.45	40.68	11.76	28.13	5.80	18.21	11.58	100.00

Another aspect of the owner-operator that has been greatly questioned is, How deeply has the union penetrated the ranks of owner-operators? It is particularly useful to examine this question on the basis of the commodity that the owner-operator regularly carries. Table 9-5 shows substantial union membership among owner-operators carrying iron and steel, heavy metal objects and machinery, motor vehicles, and general commodities. Nonrefrigerated farm products and refrigerated products are among the least organized areas. One must be cautious here about what constitutes unionization. The specific question asked on the questionnaire was whether the owner-operator was a member of a union. First, I am not sure whether the driver who answer yes was a Teamster or a member of another union. Second, many owner-operators who are Teamsters may not necessarily be operating under a Teamster contract.

I felt it was important to consider the perception of the standard of living of owner-operators who carry specific commodities. This perception of standard of living might be compared with company drivers (employees) carrying the same commodity to determine if the level of income was simply a commodity-related issue. Also, a comparison might be made with owner-operators who regularly carried other commodities.

Table 9-6 makes these comparisons. Greater proportions of the population of owner-operators who carry iron and steel, heavy metal objects and machinery, and motor vehicles reported below average standards of living. Every other category of owner-operator had greater proportions of drivers who reported high standards of living. There is some evidence to suggest that the commodity groups in which there was the greatest penetration of union membership were also the groups with the drivers who were least satisfied with their economic situation.

Table 9-5
Union Status of Owner-Operators,
Reported by Commodities Carried
(percent)

	Union Status		
Commodities Regularly Carried This Past Year	*Union*	*Nonunion*	*Total*
Iron and steel	69.6	30.4	100.00
Heavy metal objects, machinery	63.6	36.4	100.00
Motor vehicles	70.6	29.4	100.00
Farm products (not refrig.)	21.9	78.1	100.00
Refrigerated	17.5	82.5	100.00
General commodities	62.7	37.3	100.00
Household goods	74.7	35.3	100.00
Building materials	39.7	60.3	100.00
Other	51.0	49.0	100.00

Unfortunately I cannot tell if this dissatisfaction was because of unionization. But I believe that this dissatisfaction was the primary reason for union penetration.

There are reports from owner-operators of economic abuses and sharp practices by companies who use owner-operators. These alleged abuses often relate to owner-operators being required to buy insurance or fuel at prices that owner-operators believe are above the market price. Also, some drivers argue that they are forced to pay certain expenses that company employees are not required to pay. Finally, some owner-operators object to escrow accounts or deposits required by the companies they work for.

Table 9-7 examines the experience of owner-operators in each of the commodity groups relative to several practices that drivers complain of. It may seem ironic to some readers that some owner-operators complained of being required to buy fuel from the company they operate for. During the period of limited fuel allocation, "the energy crisis," many owner-operators justly complained that they were not allowed to buy fuel at any price from the companies they operated for. It is interesting that motor vehicle carriers are particularly required to buy fuel and insurance through other companies.

It is useful to compare the practices of companies toward their own employees regarding payment of violations and living expenses, as reported in table 9-8. The practices of companies toward employees regarding moving violations are not substantially different from the owner-operator experience. The one greatest difference occurs in the treatment of overweight violations. Company employees are substantially less likely to be required to make such payments, whereas nearly all owner-operators are required to do so. Since owner-operators may not control the load, it is easy to see why they are very sensitive to this practice.

The practices regarding nonpayment of motel expenses of owner-operators explains the heavy use of sleeper cabs (84 to 91 percent) reported in chapter 6.

Owner-operators were asked their attitude toward being an owner-operator. I attempted to identify drivers who were at least satisfied with their situation, while among the dissatisfied owner-operators, I tried to distinguish between those who were marginally in the industry, not willing to renew their investment in equipment, and those who definitely wanted to exit at the earliest possible opportunity. These responses are summarized in table 9-9 on the basis of commodities carried by the owner-operator.

The first point to be recognized in table 9-9 is that the majority of the owner-operators in each commodity category are at least reasonably satisfied with their situation. However, substantial portions of the owner-operators in each group are dissatisfied and many want out. Several observations may be made when tables 9-9 and 9-6 are compared. In most commodity groups, a greater proportion of drivers want out than reported below average standards of living. Also, the owner-operators who consider their standard of living above

Table 9-6
Perceptions of Standard of Living,
Reported by Commodities Carried and Type of Operation
(percent)

Commodities Regularly Carried This Past Year	Company Driver's Perceived Standard of Living					Owner-Operator's Perceived Standard of Living				
	Below Average	Average	Above Average	High	Total	Below Average	Average	Above Average	High	Total
Iron and steel	7.75	58.00	27.54	6.71	100.00	19.90	63.77	14.03	2.30	100.00
Heavy metal objects, machinery	4.28	60.78	27.32	7.62	100.00	18.72	50.42	17.45	3.40	100.00
Motor vehicles	9.00	31.28	55.45	4.27	100.00	10.00	26.00	56.00	8.00	100.00
Bulk products	4.92	30.77	58.46	5.85	100.00	a	a	a	a	a
Farm products (not refrig.)	6.23	20.15	67.03	6.59	100.00	4.40	12.09	56.04	27.47	100.00
Refrigerated	6.44	19.54	64.83	9.20	100.00	5.02	14.15	46.58	32.25	100.00
General commodities	5.71	32.67	59.55	2.07	100.00	2.81	15.20	55.72	26.27	100.00
Household goods	5.86	29.39	61.29	2.83	100.00	2.88	17.58	57.06	22.48	100.00
Building materials	6.24	27.90	60.83	5.03	100.00	1.58	14.86	59.46	24.10	100.00

[a]Sample too small to be reliable.

Table 9-7
Practices Reported by Owner-Operators,
Reported by Commodities Carried
(percent)

Commodities Regularly Carried This Past Year	Owner-Operators Required to Buy		Owner-Operators Required to Pay			Motel/ Hotel	Companies Maintain Escrow Deposit
	Fuel	*Insurance*	*Road Taxes*	*Moving Violations*	*Overweight Violations*		
Iron and steel	1.88	11.41	47.47	99.50	94.18	77.30	64.08
Heavy metal objects, machinery	4.44	13.22	56.14	99.15	91.38	84.98	60.94
Motor vehicles	14.29	18.75	27.45	98.04	90.00	100.00	29.41
Farm products (not refrig.)	4.82	12.94	50.57	97.92	85.42	90.32	22.78
Refrigerated	5.71	15.71	63.38	98.65	87.44	91.52	44.23
General commodities	4.68	14.31	64.56	98.53	85.63	91.65	65.44
Household goods	4.23	14.24	78.36	98.58	93.36	96.02	77.55
Building materials	5.54	9.22	51.86	99.78	91.41	87.19	50.68
Other	5.35	13.73	54.97	98.71	84.51	90.27	47.25

Table 9-8
Practices Reported by Company Drivers,
Reported by Commodities Carried
(percent)

	Drivers Required to Pay		
Commodities Regularly Carried This Past Year	*Moving Violations*	*Overweight Violations*	*Motel/ Hotel*
Iron and steel	90.8	17.2	17.8
Heavy metal objects, machinery	91.3	8.4	13.3
Motor vehicles	93.0	5.7	16.2
Bulk products	94.9	7.0	11.6
Farm products (not refrig.)	93.6	9.3	18.1
Refrigerated	94.2	23.5	25.2
General commodities	97.3	3.0	6.6
Livestock	84.9	9.7	29.0
Household goods	94.4	5.0	9.6
Building materials	94.3	9.5	12.8
Other	94.4	5.7	9.1

average or high are greater than the number of owner-operators who are satisfied with their owner-operator situation. So, there appear to be factors beyond standard of living operating. The owner-operator's life may not be as romantic as portrayed by the popular press and country western music. This was confirmed in their comments.

Table 9-10 addresses some of the major problems identified by owner-operators in each commodity group. Owner-operators believe that rate cutting is the greatest problem they experience. Brokers often set the rates for farm products, so pricing is out of the hands of the owner-operators. Rates of the ICC-regulated commodities are established by the carriers the owner-operators work for. This rate setting is done by independent filing by the carrier or joint filing in the rate-bureau process described in chapter 1. The owner-operators are not active participants in this process. The rates are presented to them as an accomplished fact on what the owner-operator sees as a take-it-or-leave-it basis. The only practical way for the owner-operators to demonstrate disapproval is to refuse to work at such rates, something that may be difficult to do if they are financially distressed. This supports the argument of Mike Parkhurst, the articulate publisher of the owner-operator publication *Overdrive*. He strongly argues that antitrust immunity of the rate bureaus lends strength to the process that perpetuates the financial plight of the owner-operators and institutionally excludes them as direct participants.

Table 9-9
Attitude toward Being an Owner-Operator,
Reported by Commodities Carried
(percent)

	Attitude toward Being an Owner-Operator			
Commodities Regularly Carried This Past Year	*Fine*	*Not Again*	*Want Out*	*Total*
Iron and steel	64.90	22.69	12.41	100.00
Heavy metal objects, machinery	67.25	20.09	12.66	100.00
Motor vehicles	80.39	13.72	5.89	100.00
Farm products (not refrig.)	70.22	14.89	14.89	100.00
Refrigerated	61.69	20.09	18.22	100.00
General commodities	56.54	17.87	15.59	100.00
Household goods	71.30	15.68	13.02	100.00
Building materials	69.66	18.62	11.72	100.00
Other	71.62	14.05	14.33	100.00

A relatively large proportion of owner-operators report that they are not paid in full or experience holdbacks and unauthorized deductions. This suggests possible ambiguous or misunderstood contractual agreements as well as unattractive company behavior. I am reasonably sure that "slow pay" problems in some cases are attempts by companies to minimize cash flow and conserve their own working capital at the expense of the owner-operator. In other cases, I believe that the owner-operators may be the victims of incomplete documentation or sluggish paperwork processing of larger companies. Regardless of the cause, slow pay is a significant problem when one considers how thinly financed many owner-operators are and notes the relatively prompt payment of shipping bills required under ICC regulations.

Regulatory Status

The fourth way to categorize owner-operators is according to the status they operate under: exempt, contract, or common carriers. This categorization is relevant because of potential implications for policy decisions and rule making for the ICC. For example, are practices of contract and common carriers toward their owner-operators different? How do such practices compare to those experienced by owner-operators in the exempt areas? Tables 9-11, 9-12, and 9-13 summarize owner-operator practices by regulatory status. Several differences appear in these tables. Contract carriers more frequently require their owner-operators to pay their own road taxes. This may be because the owner-operators

Table 9-10
Major Problems Experienced by Owner-Operators, Reported by Commodities Carried
(percent)

Commodities Regularly Carried This Past Year	Major Problems Experienced by Owner-Operators						
	Unauthorized Deductions	Slow Pay	Carriers Cut Rates	Holdbacks	Not Paid in Full	Finance Charges	No or False Freight Bills
Iron and steel	14.06	19.09	41.82	13.66	9.84	7.58	19.52
Heavy metal objects, machinery	20.89	26.58	39.30	16.59	23.08	9.26	20.63
Motor vehicles	15.22	19.15	32.61	13.04	15.56	9.09	9.09
Farm products (not refrig.)	21.84	28.74	37.64	24.10	15.29	17.86	23.46
Refrigerated	22.79	35.02	42.92	24.10	18.19	14.22	23.94
General commodities	16.18	34.15	23.74	25.14	20.08	12.25	13.35
Household goods	15.56	32.12	22.40	22.47	16.67	9.94	7.72
Building materials	12.70	22.30	27.78	14.01	12.62	7.30	12.41
Other	12.96	22.78	21.31	13.28	12.54	7.85	9.94

Table 9-11
Practices Reported by Owner-Operators,
Reported by Regulatory Status
(percent)

Regulatory Status	Owner-Operators Required to Buy		Owner-Operators Required to Pay				Companies Maintain Escrow Deposit
	Fuel	Insurance	Road Taxes	Moving Violations	Overweight Violations	Motel/ Hotel	
Exempt	4.7	18.6	50.0	99.0	89.0	90.0	30.2
Private	NA	NA	NA	NA	NA	NA	NA
Contract	2.1	11.6	72.0	99.3	90.8	95.1	71.2
Common	4.4	12.2	55.4	99.2	87.3	84.3	65.4

in this category do more trip leasing outside the carrier they work for. Contract carriers and common carriers more frequently require escrow accounts or deposits than exempt companies do. This is a striking difference. It may relate to the nature of the exempt business where fewer advances are made to drivers. While there are few differences between owner-operator and company driver practices on moving violations, the differences in practices regarding overweight violations are very great. The same pattern is seen with hotel bills. One interpretation is that owner-operators truly appear to act as independent subcontractors on these points. However, another interpretation is that the owner-operator may be without enough bargaining power to get a fair deal.

The problems perceived by the owner-operators regarding rate cutting, particularly in the exempt commodities, are underscored in table 9–13. It is argued that economic deregulation will help owner-operators.

There is evidence from studies made by the ICC and the Department of Transportation (DOT) that there are significantly higher levels of empty trucks (on backhauls) among the exempt carriers. One ICC study showed that 25.5 percent of exempt trucks were empty compared to 19.1 percent of ICC-regulated trucks.[2] Another study conducted by the DOT showed 30 percent and 21.6 percent empty (unspecialized) trucks in exempt and ICC-regulated operations.[3] Deregulation of trucking is not expected to stimulate primary demand, as was argued in the airline passenger market. But it might reduce barriers among classes of carriers and eliminate empty trucks from passing each other in opposite directions. In any event, it appears that there is validity in the argument of Mike Parkhurst that the present boundaries of the exempt list are narrow enough to place a disproportionate burden of the imbalance problem on the shoulders of the exempt sector and its major participants, the owner-operators.

Table 9–12
Practices Reported by Company Drivers,
Reported by Regulatory Status
(percent)

	Drivers Required to Pay		
Regulatory Status	*Moving Violations*	*Overweight Violations*	*Motel/ Hotel*
Exempt	89.7	41.4	41.4
Private	88.6	12.6	19.4
Contract	93.1	19.6	22.1
Common	96.4	3.2	7.0

Table 9-13
Major Problems Experienced by Owner-Operators,
Reported by Regulatory Status
(percent)

	Regulatory Status		
Major Problems Experienced by Owner-Operators	*Exempt*	*Contract*	*Common*
Unauthorized deductions	16.8	13.9	14.7
Slow pay	41.7	28.4	20.7
Carrier cutting rates	52.1	21.7	32.7
Holdbacks	27.5	21.0	14.4
Not paid in full	17.2	15.2	12.9
Finance charges	16.3	10.6	7.8
No or false freight bills	23.1	10.1	15.8

Do rate problems in the exempt area, as presently defined, suggest an expansion of economic troubles for truckers if more or all commodities become exempt? The answer is not clear. Some argue that the rates of present regulated commodites will be bid down, as seen among the present exempt commodities. Others argue that the rates of the presently exempt commodities are at depressed rates because this is all that shippers can afford to pay or it is necessary to compete with rail rates. They argue that presently regulated commodities might see little change in rates. A third argument is that rates on the presently regulated commodities would settle at a middle level between the two. The first scenario would please some shippers who see deregulation as a way to reduce rates. The second scenario, if true, would probably resolve many of the financial problems of the owner-operator. The third scenario might partially satisfy both, but would fall short of being a solution. The problem is that we do not know which scenario is correct.

Table 9-13 suggests that the situation of the owner-operator in the exempt industry is more problematical than in the regulated segments. While there appear to be several fruitful areas for which the ICC might consider making owner-operator rules, the major problems really fall outside the ICC's jurisdiction.

Table 9-14 examines the perceptions of owner-operators regarding the causes of their problems. Initially I determined the proportion of the owner-operators who believed they did not have problems. As might be expected when one is asked to comment on problems, few owner-operators felt that there were no problems. It is interesting to see how owner-operators feel about the proportion of rate they receive compared to the proportion retained by the carrier they work for. I expected owner-operators' resentment toward what I describe as *toll-*

ing charges for the use of ICC authorities. Nearly 50 percent of the common-carrier drivers did state that their own share of the revenue was too small. This is certainly a concern, but it was substantially lower than I expected. This may be because they have no way to judge what the services of the company are worth.

A relatively high proportion of drivers attribute blame, for owner-operator problems to "unexpected costs" and a low proportion see "poor financial management" as an important problem. What did the owner-operators mean when they responded to the question? Perhaps they were thinking of a very narrow definition of financial management such as how their equipment was "financed" and ignored or did not recognize the role of management in avoiding surprises.

Equipment Finance and Condition

Many owner-operators are under considerable economic pressure arising from their equipment financing. As seen in table 9-15, 6.8 to 25 percent of the owner-operators in each category are behind on their payments. More importantly, 1.9 to 5.2 percent are over two months late, a situation that probably makes them candidates for equipment repossession. Two observations may be

Table 9-14
Perceptions by Owner-Operators of Causes of Their Problems,
Reported by Regulatory Status
(percent)

Perception of Causes of Problems of Owner-Operators	Regulatory Status		
	Exempt	*Contract*	*Common*
No problems	2.00	3.17	3.66
Rates too low	66.00	74.29	48.45
Proportion paid to owner-operators too small	39.00	53.25	49.86
Too many owner-operators	16.00	11.35	11.55
Unexpected costs	41.00	47.41	41.27
Poor financial management	2.00	9.68	7.46
Restrictive safety regulations	16.00	16.03	12.82
ICC regulations and authorities	44.00	34.39	31.69

Note: May exceed 100 percent because of multiple causes.

based on table 9-16. First, a larger proportion of union owner-operators own paid-off equipment. This particularly occurs in the common-carrier category. Among owner-operators who finance their equipment, I found that 2.8 percent of union operators are over two months late compared to 3.3 percent for nonunion operators.

It is striking that such a high proportion of exempt drivers is over two months behind on equipment payments. One would expect that an operator under this financial pressure (the threat of loss of her or his investment in the equipment) would be likely to cut corners in operations. This is confirmed in chapter 10.

Is there a difference between the equipment financial conditions of the several types of owner-operators? Drivers who drive for themselves, the truly independent operators, are more likely to have equipment that is already paid off or current on payments if financed. (See table 9-16.) The long-term leasors are in more tenuous financial situations. The trip leasors are in much poorer financial condition. This category of owner-operators may be under the greatest pressure, jumping from one situation to another to meet financial obligations.

It has been suggested that the age of the truck influences the financial condition and attitude of the owner-operator. Table 9-17 summarizes the distribution of the ages of owner-operator trucks in the survey. Since the survey was made in the middle of the 1978 model year, that category has little meaning.

Table 9-15
Equipment Financial Status of Owner-Operators,
Reported by Union and Regulatory Status
(percent)

Equipment Financial Status	Regulatory Status			
	Exempt	Private	Contract	Common
Union Owner-Operators				
Paid off	a	10.6	29.5	21.5
Current	a	82.6	60.5	69.6
1 to 2 months late	a	4.9	7.5	6.7
>2 months late	a	1.9	2.5	2.2
Total	100.0	100.0	100.0	100.0
Nonunion Owner-Operators				
Paid off	12.5	12.0	12.6	12.4
Current	62.5	76.4	76.9	74.5
1 to 2 months late	19.8	8.9	8.0	10.2
>2 months late	5.2	2.7	2.5	2.9
Total	100.0	100.0	100.0	100.0

Table 9-16
Equipment Financial Status of Owner-Operators,
Reported by Type of Owner-Operator
(percent)

	Type of Owner-Operator		
	Drive for Self	Trip Lease	Long-Term Lease
Equipment Financial Status of All Owner-Operators			
Paid off	24.8	14.2	14.8
Current on payments	69.2	75.0	75.5
Late 1 to 2 months	4.7	7.1	7.4
Late over 2 months	1.3	3.7	2.3
Total	100.0	100.0	100.0
Equipment Financial Status of Owner-Operators Who Have Not Paid Off Equipment			
Current on payments	92.0	87.4	88.6
Late 1 to 2 months	6.2	8.3	8.7
Late over 2 months	1.8	4.3	2.7
Total	100.0	100.0	100.0

The low number of 1975 and 1976 model trucks probably represents the relatively lower number of entries and equipment replacements that occurred in the period immediately after the "energy crisis" and owner-opeator reactions of 1974.

The most positive owner-operators are those with older trucks (over seven years) and new trucks (under three years). (See table 9-18.) This probably reflects the initial enthusiasm of the more recent entrant and fewer maintenance problems of new equipment on one side, and the advantages of paid-off status and lower initial price paid for tractors in the past. As seen in table 9-19, over 42 percent of the trucks in the oldest category (over seven years) are paid off. Unfortunately, if the equipment is financed, this is also the category that has the highest proportion of owner-operators who are over two months behind on payments (5.19 percent). This suggests that it is more difficult to make payments if you have recently bought old equipment.

Does the safety of the basic tractor systems vary with age? Owner-operators believe that the youngest tractors have safest equipment, as seen in table 9-20. But it is interesting that they also seem to hold the belief that the oldest equipment, presumably well maintained, is next safest. Is this equipment really this safe, or is it simply a love generated from long-term familiarity with a piece of

Table 9-17
Model-Year Distribution of Owner-Operator Tractors

Model Year of Tractor	Age of Tractor, Years	Percentage of Total Sample	Percentage of Tractors This Age and Older
1978	0	1.42	100.00
1977	1	18.13	98.58
1976	2	8.06	80.45
1975	3	7.74	72.39
1974	4	18.60	64.65
1973	5	12.54	46.05
1972	6	8.38	33.51
1971	7	4.37	25.13
1970	8	5.64	20.76
1969	9	4.43	15.12
1968	10	1.42	10.67
1967	11	2.00	9.27
1966	12	1.74	7.27
1965	13	1.37	5.53
≤1964	≥14	4.16	4.16

Table 9-18
Attitudes toward Continuing as an Owner-Operator,
Reported by Age of Truck Operated
(percent)

Attitude toward Being an Owner-Operator	Model Year of Truck (Truck Age, Years)			
	<1971 (>7)	1971-1972 (7-6)	1973-1975 (5-3)	1976-1978 (2-0)
Fine	71.0	63.0	67.0	72.3
Want to continue but will not replace current equipment	16.9	23.4	18.2	16.2
Want out	12.1	13.6	14.8	11.5
Total	100.0	100.0	100.0	100.0

Table 9-19
Equipment Financial Status of Owner-Operator,
Reported by Age of Truck Operated
(percent)

	Model Year of Truck (Truck Age, Years)			
	<1971 (>7)	1971-1972 (7-6)	1973-1975 (5-3)	1976-1978 (2-0)
Equipment Financial Status of All Owner-Operators				
Paid off	42.4	15.0	16.0	5.2
Current on payments	51.9	76.4	77.9	86.6
Late 1 to 2 months	2.7	6.0	3.6	7.0
Late over 2 months	3.0	2.6	2.5	1.2
Total	100.0	100.0	100.0	100.0
Equipment Financial Status of Owner-Operators Who Have Not Paid Off Equipment				
Current on payments	90.1	89.9	92.7	91.4
Late 1 to 2 months	4.7	7.0	4.3	7.4
Late over 2 months	5.2	3.0	3.0	1.2
Total	100.0	100.0	100.0	100.0

equipment? Table 9-21 provides little help in explaining this. But another explanation is that perhaps newer equipment is not "aging as gracefully" as equipment did in the past.

Where does older equipment operate? The tractors operating in farm products, iron and steel, and building materials appear to be older. (See table 9-22.) The younger tractors appear in household goods, general commodities, and motor vehicles. These three commodity groups are among the fastest growing sectors. The age of the equipment may be more of a reflection of a growing market segment compared to a mature segment of the industry.

Problems and Behavior

How do owner-operators who sense particular problems behave? Table 9-23 suggests that the behavior is quite different. Owner-operators who said they had no problems showed the safest driving practices and records. As might be expected, the drivers who feel the strongest about restrictive safety practices are those who tend to exceed the driving restrictions and speed limits the most. The drivers who stated that ICC regulations and authorities are a major problem are

Table 9-20
Proportion of Owner-Operators Who Consider Their Equipment Unsafe,
Reported by Age of Truck Operated
(percent)

	Model Year of Truck (Truck Age, Years)			
Equipment System, Tractor	<1971 (>7)	1971–1972 (7–6)	1973–1975 (5–3)	1976–1978 (2–0)
Tractor				
Tires	1.0	0.4	0.7	0.2
Electrical	0.8	0.4	0.4	0.2
Brakes	1.5	2.9	0.7	1.3
Engine	1.3	1.7	1.2	0.4
Suspension	1.8	1.2	1.8	0.2

Table 9-21
Cab Work Conditions, Proportion of Owner-Operators
Who Find Each Feature to Be a Major Problem,
Reported by Age of Truck Operated
(percent)

	Model Year of Truck (Truck Age, Years)			
Item	<1971 (>7)	1971–1972 (7–6)	1973–1975 (5–3)	1976–1978 (2–0)
Noise	3.9	5.0	4.0	2.9
Vibration	4.7	3.4	7.2	5.4
Fumes	3.4	0.8	1.7	1.2
Seating	4.4	2.9	6.0	3.7
Temperature/humidity	5.2	5.5	5.7	3.7
Cleanliness	6.7	5.0	5.8	4.1

among those who most frequently did not comply with safe driving practices, received the most moving violations, and had the most reportable accidents. There appears to be an association between resentment of economic regulation and safety, an issue to be addressed in chapter 10.

Finally, what reasons are given if an owner-operator decides to quit? I would not suggest that the data in table 9-24 are representative of all owner-operators who have ever decided not to continue, since these respondents are still in the industry. However, for the drivers who were "previously owner-opera-

Table 9-22
Model Year of Owner-Operator Trucks,
Reported by Commodities Carried
(percent)

	Model Year of Truck (Truck Age, Years)				
Commodities Regularly Carried This Past Year	*<1971 (>7)*	*1971–1972 (7–6)*	*1973–1975 (5–3)*	*1976–1978 (2–0)*	*Total*
Iron and steel	24.17	17.81	38.17	19.85	100.00
Heavy metal objects, machinery	19.16	19.62	44.86	16.36	100.00
Motor vehicles	16.00	12.00	38.00	34.00	100.00
Farm products (not refrig.)	30.53	16.84	32.63	20.00	100.00
Refrigerated	15.74	11.57	40.74	31.95	100.00
General commodities	10.88	10.88	41.46	36.78	100.00
Household goods	9.53	11.33	43.06	36.26	100.00
Building materials	24.56	14.47	34.87	26.10	100.00
Other	28.46	11.75	36.03	23.76	100.00

tors" in this survey, the primary reason given for quitting as an owner-operator was financial. The category "Other" was primarily used by the drivers to describe personal reasons. The drivers who now work as company drivers showed a higher proportion giving up being an owner-operator for financial reasons. The drivers who said they returned to being an owner-operator showed fewer financial reasons and increased personal reasons. Presumably, after resolving their problems, they elected to return to being an owner-operator.

Summary

The owner-operators who drive for themselves show a more positive attitude about their standard of living. They appear to have developed their own means for arranging backhauls, and over 75 percent of them are satisfied with their situation.

There is deepest union penetration among owner-operators in the parts of the ICC-regulated industry where the standard of living is the lowest. But it could also be said that there is still the lowest perception of standard of living where union penetration is the greatest. This is the reverse of what was reported among union company employees.

Low rates are the most frequently mentioned reason given by owner-operators for their troubles. This was particularly true among the exempt owner-operators. Owner-operators are not particularly concerned about too many other owner-operators. While there are some complaints about the portion of the rate

Table 9-23
Driving Performance and Records of Owner-Operators,
Reported by Their Perceptions of the Causes of Their Problems

Perceptions of Causes of Problems of Owner-Operators	Average Cruising Speed, mph	Regularly Drive Beyond 10-Hour Limit, percent˙	Reportable Accidents per 100,000 Miles	Moving Violations per 100,000 Miles
No problems	57.6	12.8	0.3	0.6
Rates too low	60.8	29.1	0.3	0.9
Proportion paid to owner-operators too small	60.9	26.8	0.3	0.8
Too many owner-operators	60.4	28.3	0.4	0.8
Unexpected costs	60.5	26.4	0.4	0.8
Poor financial management	60.3	32.0	0.4	0.6
Restrictive safety practices	62.0	39.1	0.3	0.9
ICC regulations and authorities	61.6	37.2	0.4	1.0

Table 9-24
Reasons for Giving Up Being an Owner-Operator,
Reported by Current Driving Status
(percent)

Reason for Giving Up Being an Owner-Operator in the Past	All Drivers Who Have Previously Been Owner-Operators	How Driving Now	
		Company	Owner-Operator
Hassle	13.38	12.86	14.72
Loss of interest	5.84	6.16	5.19
Mechanical problems	2.37	2.32	2.16
Lack of business	8.17	8.54	7.58
Financial	49.67	51.52	43.29
Other	20.57	18.67	27.06
Total	100.00	100.00	100.00

that the owner-operator is paid, they are not as great as one might expect. Unexpected costs are seen as a problem, but owner-operators do not associate surprises with poor financial management.

A high proportion of owner-operators are late on their payments. Compared to owner-operators in general, almost twice as many of the owner-operators working as exempt carriers are over two months behind on their payments.

The owner-operators with relatively old trucks and new trucks are among the most satisfied. These attitudes appear to be related to paid-off status for the older trucks and initial enthusiasm and reduced maintenance cost of the new trucks.

Finally, approximately half of the drivers in the survey who previously gave up being an owner-operator gave financial reasons as their motivation.

Notes

1. Interstate Commerce Commission, *Public Response to Proposals for Improving Motor-Carrier Regulation*, Ex-Parte No. MC-113, December 1977.

2. Charles River Associates Inc., *Potential Fuel Conservation Measures By Motor-Carriers in the Intercity Freight Market* (Washington, D.C.: Federal Energy Administration, 1977), appendix A, p. A-35.

3. Ibid., A-41.

10 _ Implications of Economic Regulation

The interstate motor-carrier industry is regulated in two ways. The first form of regulation deals with how trucks are operated and covers such subjects as speed, load size, truck size, hours of service, and other aspects of truck driving. The second form of regulation, the part that falls under the ICC, is economic. This regulation deals with entry, routes, commodities, rates, finances, and exit. These two forms of regulation were originally both under the jurisdiction of the ICC. However, the operating and safety regulation was transferred to the Department of Transportation when the department was created. This separation reflects the generally held belief that these two aspects of the industry can be successfully unbundled.

Many motor-carrier managers are of the opinion that there is a connection between economic regulation and the extent of compliance with safety regulation. Most trucking managers I have met strongly believe that the exempt segment of the industry is relatively undisciplined regarding safety. Similarly, I had heard that owner-operators who are under relatively less control of the company are more likely to treat safety regulation more lightly than company drivers. This study provided an opportunity to observe whether these conditions did exist.

Association of Economic Regulation and Safety Compliance

Table 10-1 is a summary of safety compliance and performance of company drivers and owner-operators of each regulatory status. In most categories there was little difference between owner-operators and company drivers in the exempt sector. It is not possible to report this comparison among the private carriers since owner-operators in private carriage are generally illegal operations. However, private-carrier company drivers appear to have better safety compliance than their exempt counterparts.

The company drivers of the ICC-regulated for-hire carriers (contract and common) show even greater compliance. In fact, the company drivers of the common carriers, the most closely economically regulated carriers of the industry, report the highest compliance and best performance.

It is clear that these differences are not as evident among the owner-operators. Some association between degree of economic regulation and safety compliance and performance exists among the owner-operators. However, the differences among categories of owner-operators is much less pronounced.

Table 10-1
Driver Safety Compliance and Performance,
Reported by Type of Operation and Regulatory Status
(percent)

	Regulatory Status			
	Exempt	*Private*	*Contract*	*Common*
Average Cruising Speed, mph				
Owner-Operators	62.6	NA	61.0	60.3
Company drivers	63.0	61.7	59.4	58.9
Drivers Who Regularly Use Multiple Logbooks, percent				
Owner-Operators	27.4	NA	10.2	11.9
Company drivers	32.1	9.6	4.9	1.8
Drivers Who Regularly Misrepresent Logbooks, percent				
Owner-Operators	44.9	NA	33.6	33.9
Company drivers	39.3	29.4	20.3	4.3
Drivers Who Regularly Exceed 10-Hour Limit, percent				
Owner-Operators	43.9	NA	27.2	24.0
Company drivers	46.0	25.1	13.1	2.5
Moving Violations per 100,000 Miles				
Owner-Operators	1.3	NA	0.7	0.8
Company drivers	1.3	0.9	0.8	0.4
Reportable Accidents per 100,000 Miles				
Owner-Operators	0.7	NA	0.3	0.3
Company drivers	0.2	0.2	0.3	0.2

Question of Cause and Effect

Is there a cause-and-effect relationship between economic regulation and safety compliance? That they are associated in a statistical fashion does not necessarily demonstrate a causal relationship. The association could be accidental. However, given the strength of the data, I doubt that this is the case.

One explanation is that safety compliance and economic regulation are related to one or more other factors that are not captured in table 10-1.

In earlier chapters it was observed that safety compliance and performance were also associated with age and union membership. Table 10-2 examines the extent to which the phenomena I observed could be explained by these two

Table 10-2
Proportion of Company Drivers Who Regularly
Exceed the 10-Hour Driving Limit,
Reported by Age of Driver and Union Status
(percent)

	Regulatory Status			
	Exempt	*Private*	*Contract*	*Common*
Age of Driver				
<25	a	a	39.1	17.4
25–50	48.5	26.6	15.0	3.1
>50	a	16.1	1.8	0.8
Union Status				
Union	a	14.2	6.3	1.7
Nonunion	52.1	33.3	32.3	23.4

[a]Sample too small to be reliable.

variables. For example, among company drivers, it is seen that age is a significant factor. In each category of regulatory status, in so far as data were available,
it appeared that compliance with the 10-hour driving limitation is associated
with the age of the driver. However, after controlling for age, the pattern of association of safety compliance with regulatory status is still evident. To what
extent is union membership associated with compliance? Again, in each category
of regulatory status it appears that compliance with the 10-hour driving limitation is associated with union membership. But the association of safety compliance with regulatory status exists.

I am not confident that age, union status, and economic regulation are
truly independent variables.

I do not believe that it is accidental that union drivers are older than nonunion drivers. The strong seniority system that is part of the fabric of union
organization definitely contributes to the older average age of union drivers.

Similarly, I believe that economic regulation and union organization in the
trucking industry are related. For example, among the respondents to the survey, it is clear that union penetration among the company drivers is greatest in
common carriers, followed by contract carriers, private carriers, and finally
exempt carriers. (See table 10-3.) It has been argued that the strength of the IBT
is closely related to a combination of industrywide bargaining and the rate-mak-
ing process. This process is primarily associated with the common carriers, and
would explain the strength of the union among the respondents who were
company drivers with that type of carrier. Also, I suspect that unionization may
also be related to the size of the company. Although the IBT is willing to organ-

Table 10-3
Proportion of Drivers Who Are Union Members,
Reported by Type of Operator and Regulatory Status
(percent)

	Regulatory Status			
Union Members	*Exempt*	*Private*	*Contract*	*Common*
Owner-Operators	15.3	NA	63.2	65.3
Company drivers	18.0	44.8	73.8	96.6

ize a company with as few as two drivers, it is more typical that organizing attention has been focused on larger workforces. Therefore, it might be argued that the degree of union penetration in each category is simply a surrogate for size of workforce. One extension of this line of reasoning is that economic regulation has led to larger companies, which, in turn, have simultaneously been more likely (1) to be organized and (2) to be more responsible regarding compliance with safety regulation.

It would have been desirable for the survey to capture the size of the company the driver worked for. An early version of the questionnaire included this question, but it was found that most drivers had very little knowledge of the dimensions of their employer. Rather than indicate fleet size or revenues, drivers simple answered "do not know."

I am suspicious of the variable "size of company" totally explaining compliance with safety regulation. In fact, I believe that many of the private-carrier drivers worked for very large companies. Many of the contract carriers are relatively small. While most exempt carriers are small, I do not see strong evidence that the size of company is the only or even primary influence.

Truckline managers often offer another explanation. They believe that economic regulation has led to a more responsible attitude toward safety compliance among companies in that category. They refer to the requirement that a carrier be "fit, willing, and able" to provide service before the ICC grants operating authority. Most managers partly equate fitness with demonstrated safety compliance and sincerely feel that being found unfit will preclude granting of new or suspension of existing ICC authorities. This perception is widely held among managers, but it is difficult to demonstrate that this is, in fact, the practice of the ICC. However, if the perception that the ICC behaves this way leads to self-enforcement of safety procedures, then it is effective. It is clear that drivers who wish to avoid compliance are able to do so at will. The effectiveness of external enforcement is questionable when nearly half the drivers in some segments of the industry regularly ignore basic safety procedures, as reported in table 10-1.

Trapped by Economics: A Catch 22

What explanation is offered by the drivers? Many of the owner-operators who stated that they did not comply with safe driving practices added that they were very concerned that they found themselves in such a situation. They were concerned about the risks they found they had to take, and no drivers suggested pride in the situation. They stated fears about the safety of others as well as themselves. But this was the only way they could "make ends meet" financially. They sincerely wanted help. Simply stated, many said they had to ignore safety procedures because the procedures hampered their productivity, and they could not afford them financially. For example, drivers who regularly exceeded the 10-hour driving limitation were asked to list all the reasons they had for doing so. As seen in table 10-4, "Need the money" and "Unrealistic schedules" were the two most frequently mentioned reasons. As discovered in the comments made in the questionnaires, the unrealistic schedules were usually caused by a need for money as well. These economic pressures are very consistent with the distressed financial status reported by owner-operators in table 9-15. One driver summarized the feelings of many of the drivers when he commented, "I cannot affort to drive at the speed limit or stop after 10 hours."

It appears that economic regulation has permitted revenues that are sufficient to allow safer operations. Similarly, unionization may have led to labor insistence that a sufficient portion of this revenue be realized by the driver so that he or she can afford to be safe.

Perhaps the economic plight, and apparent subsequent safety problems, among exempt drivers is related to their exclusion from regulated traffic. As asked in chapter 9, Will deregulation change the economics of the situation?

What we seem to observe is an economic situation that traps owner-operators into unsafe practices to improve productivity to meet financial obligations. If compliance with the speed limits, drivers' hour restrictions, and other requirements is necessary, then we are achieving productivity in a socially unacceptable way. If compliance is not necessary, then why do we needlessly constrict the productivity of those who comply?

The cost of endangering the other users of the highway system is not being included in the free market pricing. I have noted before, "It seems unlikely that current economic regulation is a cost-effective means of promoting highway safety."[1] But other enforcement methods presently being used do not appear to be strong enough to force compliance to the necessary level on a basis of broad participation, so the marketplace must accept the costs in higher rates. If there were universal compliance, there would be no competitive advantage, since all would have similar costs.

Ministry of Transport annual fitness examinations, which consider accident records and operating and compliance violations, together with vehicle inspec-

Table 10–4
Reasons for Exceeding 10-Hour Driving Limits,
Reported by Drivers Who Regularly Exceed the Limit
(percent)

Reasons for Regularly Exceeding the 10-Hour Driving Limit	Company Drivers				Owner-Operators			
	Exempt	*Private*	*Contract*	*Common*	*Exempt*	*Private*	*Contract*	*Common*
Unrealistic schedule	40.0	37.4	45.2	44.8	46.5	NA	38.4	38.5
Bad weather	25.0	29.0	32.3	39.2	32.6	NA	44.5	39.1
Road conditions	20.0	17.8	19.4	24.5	20.9	NA	36.4	24.9
Breakdowns	22.5	18.7	25.8	25.3	20.9	NA	25.3	17.2
Stopping to eat or rest	7.5	12.2	8.1	8.4	4.7	NA	17.3	12.4
Need the money	47.5	37.4	59.7	42.0	51.2	NA	66.7	64.5
Instructed to do so	30.0	29.0	27.4	32.9	18.6	NA	17.3	13.6
Other	42.5	30.5	35.5	26.6	37.2	NA	32.7	36.1

tions, have served this function in the deregulated trucking industry in the United Kingdom.

However, the great question to be answered is, How can we construct an economic environment that permits, and even promotes, safe operations? It is not clear that deregulation proposals accomplish this, and there is a strong possiblity that some deregulation without other measures could place the owner-operator and exempt carriers in a worse position while bringing safety havoc to the highways.

Summary

Safety and operating regulation have been separated from economic regulation in the motor-carrier industry. Motor-carrier managers have long argued that the compliance with safety regulations, such as hours of service and speed, is poorer in the sectors of the industry that are exempt from economic regulation. This study supports this argument, even controlling for age of drivers and union membership. However, it is not clear that there is a simple causal relationship between economic regulation and safety compliance. It might be that regulated companies are larger, which might cause them to be more responsible.

The drivers explain their lack of compliance as a short-term economic necessity. When asked, they strongly answered that they ignore safety laws because they need the money.

Economic regulation appears to provide a level of revenue that is sufficient to allow companies to comply, and the union appears to be strong enough to demand it. In the present enforcement environment, the free market, as typified by the exempt segment, prices service below a level that allows for safe operation. Productivity is being gained at a social cost that cannot be assessed by the individual driver and under economic pressures that are unreasonable.

Note

1. Quoted without citation in *The Impact on Small Communites of Motor Carriage Regulatory Revision* (Washington D.C.: U.S. Senate, Committee on Commerce, Science, and Transportation, June 1978), p. 139.

11 Concluding Remarks

Working Conditions, Standards of Living, and Equipment

I found that most of the professional intercity truck drivers who participated in the study found their profession and work conditions to be good, and many drivers were very positive about their situation. Among company drivers approximately 98 percent of union and 84.5 percent of nonunion drivers believed that they made at least average standards of living. Only 16.8 percent of union and 9.4 percent of nonunion company drivers believed their companies had little or no concern for them and their working conditions. Compared to many other groups of U.S. workers, I believe these are relatively high levels of satisfaction.

The owner-operators showed a somewhat different pattern. While most felt satisfied by their situation, as many as one quarter of some categories of owner-operators were late on their equipment finance payments. Approximately one quarter of all owner-operators believed they had a below average standard of living. Research in 1974 to 1975 suggested that the owner-operators were willing to make the financial trade for independence. This does not appear to be as true today. Apparently the expectations of the owner-operator are rising. Approximately 15 percent of the owner-operators studied want out, even at a sacrifice, and a like number do not plan to replace their current equipment. This is not the same view of the world we saw in 1975 when Maister and I studied owner-operators. In the present study I found a diminished number of entries into the field and increased hostility toward the practices of some carriers they work for.

The drivers are quite tolerant of their work conditions and equipment. The youngest and oldest drivers appear to have the fewest complaints. Equipment safety is rising as a major complaint among company drivers. Perception and expectations of equipment conditions are coming apart. I found serious concern, particularly among the union drivers.

This concern regarding equipment is focused on brakes, suspensions, engines, and trailers. The degree of focus on specific equipment systems strengthens the validity of the drivers' concerns. These are not rantings of malcontent employees who complain about everything. They are not the uninformed complaints of inexperienced or job-hopping drivers. They come from the most experienced and highest seniority drivers.

To the extent that drivers have disagreements with their company or have perceptions of their company's low concern for drivers, they appear to be related to safety of equipment.

117

Suitability of Drivers for Driving: Physical Condition and Training

I found no evidence that drivers had health or physical conditions that were sub-stantially debilitating or particularly different for similar age groups in the popu-lation at large. There were higher incidence of back problems and hernias, which were probably related to earlier work as dock or warehouse employees. Some evidence of more kidney and hemorrhoid problems was seen. This may be rela-ted to riding problems. There was a suggestion of more headaches and nervous-ness among drivers, but it was not seen as critical. There is certainly no evidence to support the conclusion that drivers become owner-operators because of poorer physical or health conditions. If anything, owner-operators tended to be in better physical condition than their company driver counterparts. In general, it appears that the truck driver is fairly healthy and physically well suited for his or her work.

The finding I did not expect was the difference in age distributions among the various categories of operations and industry segments. The exempt segment has relatively young drivers, with a striking number below 25 years old. Common carriers appear to have few young drivers as employees, but are quite willing to accept them as owner-operators. Indeed, it appears that contrary to my belief that owner-operators tended to be the senior drivers of the industry, they are generally younger than company drivers. They are not necessarily the older company employee who has put enough savings aside to become an inde-pendent operator. The evidence supports the argument that these are the younger drivers who are attempting to break into the industry.

As a group, older drivers are more likely to comply with safety regulations and observe operating rules. This pays off with substantially fewer moving viola-tions and reportable accidents per year for older drivers.

The majority of truck drivers have had no formal driver training. While there is a trend toward increased formal training, nearly half of the drivers under 25 years, the most highly trained age group, still do not report such training. There is some evidence of a trend toward increased use of company-sponsored and private programs. Most formal training programs deal with such formal topics as Department of Transportation regulation, but many fail to cover such subjects as defensive or emergency driving. Nearly 87 percent of the drivers who said they regularly handle hazardous materials also report that they have not received formal training on the subject. Finally, there is no evidence that the present formal training is producing safer drivers. These formally trained drivers are more likely to ignore the 10-hour driving limitation, drive faster, and have more reportable accidents per 100,000 miles driven. While the lower average age of the formally trained drivers accounts for part of this, it is clear that formal training is not producing safer drivers on the highway.

Differences in Behavior and Attitude of Drivers
Carrying Different Commodities

Too often observations are made about the trucking industry as if it were homogeneous. The drivers who operate in each segment as employees and owner-operators have very substantially different attitudes and behavior. For example, owner-operators in iron and steel, as well as in heavy metal objects and machinery, take a dim view of their standard of living. Yet owner-operators carrying some farm products, refrigerated products, or general commodities have very positive views. While owner-operators carrying motor vehicles were not particularly positive about their standards of living, they were among the most positive in their attitudes about being owner-operators.

The group of commodities that I had the most concern about was hazardous materials because of their potential danger to drivers and others. In fact, the drivers who most frequently carried such products drove at the lowest average speeds, had the best compliance with safety rules, and had the best record on moving violations. They tended to be more experienced. Their health was no different from that of drivers of similar age.

The drivers who regularly carried hazardous materials had perceived that their equipment was relatively unsafe. It is difficult to determine whether this was based on physical facts or reflected supersensitivity of the drivers. But, approximately 20 percent of these drivers felt their tractor brakes were unsafe. Their concern is to be commended, but how should we view their employers' tolerance of such conditions?

Hazardous-materials drivers do report a greater tendency to doze, even though they have one of the best records of compliance with the 10-hour driving limitation. This, coupled with higher incidence of headaches and nervous problems, suggest higher stress levels among these drivers. This raises the question of whether the 10-hour limitation might be too liberal for such operations. These drivers do not believe that their standard of living is significantly higher for this type of work and strain.

Drugs, Pep Pills, Alcohol, and Other Substances

Drivers' responses indicated use of alcohol that was significantly lower than the average of the general population over age 18. However, between 1.6 and 7.5 percent of the drivers (ranging from the oldest to the youngest age groups) indicated that they believe they can drive satsifactorily without waiting after drinking.

Contrary to the stories heard on the road and in truck stops, there seemed to be relatively low use of pep pills. However, over 10 percent of the exempt drivers and 4.7 percent of all drivers under age 25 said they used them regularly. The use of pep pills is primarily concentrated among drivers who regularly exceed the 10-hour driving limitation, which is hardly surprising. There was little evidence of regular use of narcotics or marijuana reported by drivers.

Safety Compliance and Economic Regulation

The observations of experienced motor-carrier managers that there is substantially better compliance with safety and operating rules in the ICC-regulated sector were confirmed. Compliance with speed limits, log book procedures, and hours-of-service rules were highest among company employees in the highly regulated common-carrier segment and lowest in the exempt segment. This compliance was not as strict among owner-operators in the service of common carriers, but it is clear that they do not operate under the same level of control as employees.

Part of the higher degree of compliance seems to be related to the older average age of drivers in the common carriers. Also, part seems to be related to unionization. However, there is also some complex interlinkage among economic regulation, size of company, union organziation, and average age of driver. Each of these factors seems to contribute to safety rule compliance, and they all tend to occur together, perhaps in a causal relationship.

While company employees of common carriers may show better safety compliance to operating rules than their owner-operator or exempt counterparts, it is not clear that they believe their equipment is as safe. Owner-operators believe their equipment is safer. While this may be a perception, it has been partly corroborated by Department of Transportation roadside inspections. However, these inspections actually indicated that the exempt equipment was just *slightly* better on some equipment systems. Given the higher frequency of accidents caused by driver error, road conditions, and dozing, compared to equipment malfunction, I am more concerned with speed and driver fatigue.

Is the relationship between economic regulation and safety compliance causal? Economic regulation does result in larger carriers than exist in the exempt area. Motor-carrier managers believe and act as if the ICC is fulfilling its mandate to ensure that carriers under its jurisdiction are fit, willing, and able. Economic regulation has maintained an orderly and stable market which has provided sufficient revenues to carriers for them to afford to operate in compliance with the rules. While it is difficult to confirm a causal relationship, any action, legislative or administrative, that alters the current regulatory structure has the potential of destroying the current self-regulation of safety compliance. Since conventional enforcement methods have proved inadequate, one wonders what counter-move can be made to maintain this precarious balance?

As a final concluding note, I would like to include a comment made by one driver: "You know I really like to drive trucks. It's a great life. I'd work for nothing as long as I had a good truck and trailer and a good run. But don't tell my boss about being willing to work for nothing."

Appendix A
Glossary of Motor-
Carrier Industry
Terminology

Arranger An individual who arranges exempt loads for owner-operators (and others). These are usually small (one-person) operations, and the arranger charges a flat fee, rather than a percentage of the revenue from the load. See *Broker*.

Backhaul The return journey, usually back to a home base, but also taken to mean the (loaded) journey between the destination of one trip and the origin of the next.

BMCS Bureau of Motor Carrier Safety, Federal Highway Administration, U.S. Department of Transportation.

Break-bulk To separate a composite load into individual shipments and route to different destinations.

Broker Someone who arranges exempt loads for owner-operators (and others). These operations are larger than those of the typical arranger, and a broker usually charges a percentage of the revenue from the load as a fee.

Class I Motor Carriers Common or contract motor carriers of property that have average gross operating revenues of $3 million or more annually from motor-carrier operations (prior to 1974, more than $1 million).

Class II Motor Carriers Common or contract motor carriers of property that have average gross operating revenues of $500,000 or more, but under $3 million annually from motor-carrier operation (prior to 1974, between $300,000 and $1 million).

Class III Motor Carriers Common or contract motor-carriers of property that have average gross operating revenues of less than $500,000 annually from motor-carrier operation (prior to 1974, less than $300,000).

Commodity Any article of commerce. Goods shipped.

Common Carrier A transportation business that offers service to the general public. Interstate common carriers must hold a franchise issued by the Interstate Commerce Commission that limits service to a specific geographical area.

Contract Carrier A transportation business that offers service to a designated (small) group of customers. Interstate contract carriers must hold a franchise by the Interstate Commerce Commission.

Deadheading Running empty to relocate equipment.

Dispatching The scheduling and control of truck operations.

DOT   U.S. Department of Transportation.

Enroute   On the way.

Exempt Commodities   Those commodities whose interstate movement by truck is not subject to regulation by the ICC.

FASH   Fraternal Association of Steel Haulers, an owner-operator organization.

Freight   Any commodity being transported.

Gypsy   An owner-operator. Also used to denote an owner-operator working in exempt commodities, or one who is prepared to travel anywhere in the continental United States.

IBT   International Brotherhood of Teamsters.

Interstate Commerce Act   The act of Congress regulating the practices, rates, and rules of transportation companies enaged in handling interstate traffic.

Interstate Commerce Commission (ICC)   The federal body charged with enforcement of acts of Congress affecting interstate commerce.

Intrastate Traffic   Traffic having origin, destination, and entire transportation within the same state.

Irregular-Route Carrier   A motor carrier that primarily provides service within an area or between areas rather than between specific points. Because of this less structured route approach, irregular-route carriers usually concentrate on truckload freight.

Less Than Truckload (LTL)   A quantity of freight less than that required for the application of a truckload rate; typically less than 10,000 pounds.

Line Haul   Movement of freight between cities, excluding pickup and delivery service.

Log Book   A book carried by truck drivers; required by ICC regulations, which contains daily records of hours worked, routes, and so on.

Owner-Operator   An individual who operates his or her own truck.

Permanent Lease   A lease of at least 30 days whereby owner-operators lease themselves and their equipment to a regulated motor carrier.

Point of Origin   The terminal at which freight is received from the shipper.

Power Unit   A truck or tractor.

Private Carrier   A company that operates its own trucks to transport its own freight.

PROD   Professional Drivers Council.

Rate   The charge for transporting freight.

Rating   Determination of the correct legal rate for a shipment.

Reefer   A refrigerated trailer.

Regular-Route Carrier   A motor carrier that primarily provides service between fixed points over defined routes. Because of this structure, regular-route carriers often concentrate on LTL freight.

Reportable Accident   An accident involving property damage greater than $200 and/or personal injury.

Rig   A truck, tractor, or tractor-trailer combination.

Semitrailer   Truck trailer equipped with one or more axles and constructed so the front end rests upon a truck tractor.

Sleeper   A tractor or truck with a sleeping compartment.

Terminal   A building for the handling and temporary storage of freight pending transfer between locations.

Ton-Mile   One ton carried one mile. A measure of the output or work done in transportation operations.

Tractor   A motor vehicle designed primarily for pulling trailers.

Trailer   Freight-carrying vehicle designed to be pulled by a tractor.

Trip Lease   A lease arrangement between an owner-operator and a regulated carrier covering only one trip.

Truck   A motor vehicle designed to carry freight.

Truckload (TL)   Quantity of freight required to fill a truck. When used in connection with freight rates, the quantity of freight necessary to qualify a shipment for a truckload rate; usually over 10,000 pounds.

Appendix B
Methodology

The development of the DRVRS data base began as a project sponsored by Trucking Activites, Inc., as a public service and educational activity. The initial purpose of establishing the data base was to create a facility to study the safety records and driving practices of over-the-road drivers in various segments of the intercity trucking industry. It was found that data for such research were often not consistently captured by state and federal agencies. Also, there was usually no attempt to categorize the type of carrier (that is, exempt, private, contract, or common) or the type of operation (owner-operator or company driver) the driver worked in. This data problem precluded several types of analysis.

My purpose was to build a data base of such a large size that it would be possible to examine the behavior, attitudes, and performance of very specifically defined subpopulations.

The task was to create a means of distributing a vast number of questionnaires to such a broad sampling of drivers and secure candid responses over a very brief period. The plan was to allow the questionnaries in the field no more than four weeks, to prevent special interest groups from organizing to "stuff the ballot box" on certain issues.

A total of 65,000 questionnaires was distributed as follows: 4,000 direct mail, 30,000 through truck stops, and 30,000 through trucklines. The remaining 1,000 questionnaires were used for mailing to truckline presidents and organizations to obtain cooperation and support for the program.

Support of the nationwide distribution was provided by several groups. The Regular Common Carrier Conference provided all printing. This organization also acted as a clearing house to handle the shipment of questionnaires to participating trucklines. Union 76 Truckstops distributed questionnaires in a one-week period through 300 locations throughout the United States. Financial help and mailing lists provided by Trucking Activities, Inc., supported the direct mailing of questionnaires to the homes of owner-operators. Financial support for out-of-pocket costs for data processing and return postage was provided by the International Brotherhood of Teamsters and the Association of American Railroads. Facilities and support of transportation research at Harvard University are supported by the UPS Foundation.

The questionnaire, shown in figure B-1, detailed and addressed several sensitive issues of illegal operation, financial status, and personal questions. It was vital that confidentiality be maintained. Each questionnaire was distributed with a return-postage envelope addressed to a post office box. This would ensure that answers would remain anonymous. Approximately 200 questionnaires were collected by dispatchers or management of some trucklines and mailed directly in packages. All these questionnaires, while not being remarkably different, were excluded from the sample as a precaution against possible tampering.

I carefully declined offers of trade and labor organizations to publicize the questionnaire and the program. I chose to do this to minimize influencing respondents. However, given the rather vague statement of the purpose in the questionnaire (see figure B-1), it was to be expected that some drivers would want to know more about what the objectives were and why the survey was being conducted. Letters from drivers in this regard were answered by simply stating that I was interested in a "better understanding of the safety records, driving practices, and attitudes of the U.S. truck driver in a variety of segments of the industry." I specifically avoided stating any hypotheses I intended to test or issues I hoped to examine to avoid communicating any predisposition or bias.

I received over 12,000 questionnaires, of which 10,500 arrived within the time frame we allowed for inclusion in the sample, January 1978. After checking and coding, I had 9,630 usable questionnaires.

Approximately 25 percent of the questionnaires included comments beyond the formal questions asked. Half of these comments, often signed with a CB handle, included some statement to the effect of thanking us for providing an opportunity for the driver to state opinions. Nearly every questionnaire was fully completed and useful. I believe this is attributable to the careful pretesting of the form to be sure that questions were understandable and trucking terms used were not ambiguous or did not have different meanings in each region. Less than 100 questionnaires out of 10,500 were insincere or attempts at low humor. Several hundred drivers provided their names, but I was careful to remove such identification before data processing. Several dozen owner-operators offered to let the researchers "ride" with them for a better understanding of the life and working conditions of the driver. Hours were spent on the telephone talking to drivers who called my office at Harvard University.

The intention of the survey was to build a data base that had significant samples of a wide variety of types of trucking operations and drivers. From this data base, I could compare the safety records, driving practices, and attitudes of individual drivers. It was not intended that the returns from this questionnaire be used to construct an estimate of the size and mixture of the total population of truck drivers in the United States.

The survey was intended to be "stratified" rather than a "probability" sampling. I have included the representation of questionnaires by several categories in tables B-1 through B-3. These figures are intended to indicate the size of the data base, and are not meant to suggest that this reflects the relative size of each segment in the population of U.S. truck drivers.

Figure B-1
Truck Driver Survey Questionnaire

Harvard University, Graduate School of Business Administration

George F. Baker Foundation

D. Daryl Wyckoff *Associate Professor*

The truck driver is vital to America. Unfortunately drivers are often not heard. We are conducting a survey of thousands of truck drivers in the United States to learn more about their life, work, and economic condition. These questions will take several minutes to answer, but your help is greatly appreciated. *Skip any questions* you don't know how to answer or *don't care to answer.* We don't want to know who you are, but we want to know *your story.* Truthful answers may help you or other drivers. *Don't pull any punches,* we want to give a *true picture* of the truck drivers of the United States as they see it.

I. ABOUT YOU

1. Age, at most recent birthday: _____ years old
2. Years driving heavy duty trucks professionally_____ years
3. Years driving for present company (or self): _____ years
4. Are you a member of a union? ☐ Yes ☐ No
5. Sex ☐ Male ☐ Female
6. Are you married? ☐ Yes ☐ No ☐ Does Not Apply
7. Does your spouse work? ☐ Yes ☐ No
8. Did you attend a drivers school? ☐ Yes ☐ No
   If you attended drivers school, which type? Check all that apply
   a. ☐ Company b. ☐ Union run c. ☐ Service (Army, Navy, etc.) d. ☐ Private e. ☐ Other, please explain
   _____
9. If you attended driver's school, which of these items *were covered* in your formal training? Check all that apply
   a. ☐ Handling hazardous material b. ☐ Emergency driving
   c. ☐ Defensive driving d. ☐ Truck license and permits
   e. ☐ Hours of service and driver's logs f. ☐ D.O.T. safety regulations g. ☐ Cargo loading and securing
   h. ☐ Vehicle maintenance i. ☐ Vehicle inspection
   j. ☐ First aid k. ☐ Accident reporting l. ☐ Conduct at scene of accident m. ☐ I.C.C. regulations
10. Do you have a valid driver's or chauffeur's license for the type of vehicle you drive? Check only one. ☐ Yes ☐ No ☐ Not sure
11. Do you have any of the following? Check all that apply.
    a. ☐ Visual problems b. ☐ Hearing problems c. ☐ Hernia
    d. ☐ Back problems e. ☐ Hemorrhoid/piles
    f. ☐ Ulcers or stomach problems g. ☐ Diabetes
    h. ☐ Kidney problems i. ☐ High blood pressure
    j. ☐ Low blood pressure k. ☐ Heart problems
    l. ☐ Epilepsy m. ☐ Nervous problems
    n. ☐ Varicose veins o. ☐ Frequent headaches
12. Have you ever had your driver's license suspended or revoked?
    ☐ No ☐ Yes If yes, for what reasons? a. ☐ Speeding
    b. ☐ Driving while intoxicated c. ☐ Accumulated record
    d. ☐ Not having insurance e. ☐ Reckless driving
    f. ☐ Accident(s) g. ☐ Other, explain

13. How many *reportable accidents* have you been involved in during the past *year* (personal injury and/or more than $200 property damage?) About _____ accidents.
14. How many *unreportable accidents* have you been involved in during the past *year?* About _____ accidents.
15. How many moving traffic violations have you been ticketed for while driving a truck during the past *year?*
    About _____ violations.
16. Do you have a valid DOT/BMCS doctor's certificate? Check only one. ☐ Yes ☐ No ☐ Not sure
17. How many months ago was your last doctor's examination?
    About _____ months.
18. What state are you based in?_____ state.
19. In the past year, did your driving income provide
    ☐ High standard of living ☐ Above average living
    ☐ Average living ☐ Below average living

II. FOR WHOM DO YOU OPERATE

1. What type of motor carrier do you work for? Check one.
   ☐ *Private carrier* (a company which transports its own goods or materials such as baking company, oil company, soft drink bottler, etc.)
   ☐ *Exempt carrier* (neither I nor my employer is required to have an ICC or "MC" number because we handle exempt commodities such as fish, fresh agricultural products, air freight, newspapers)
   ☐ *Regulated interstate common carrier*
   ☐ *Regulated interstate contract carrier*
   ☐ *Agricultural Cooperative*
   ☐ *Regulated intrastate* (all one state) *carrier* (I operate only within one state.) State_____
   ☐ Other_____
2. What one answer best describes you? I drive ☐ Between cities (over 50 miles apart) ☐ Between cities and within one local area ☐ Within one local area (50 miles)
3. Approximately how many miles do you drive per year
   _____ mi./year

4. What products have you typically carried this past year?

	Never	Occasionally	Regularly
a. Iron and Steel	☐	☐	☐
b. Heavy metal objects, machinery	☐	☐	☐
c. Motor vehicles	☐	☐	☐
d. Bulk products in tanks	☐	☐	☐
e. Farm products (not refrig)	☐	☐	☐
f. Refrigerated	☐	☐	☐
g. General commodities	☐	☐	☐
h. Livestock	☐	☐	☐
i. Household goods	☐	☐	☐
j. Building materials	☐	☐	☐
k. Other	☐	☐	☐

5. Are the products you carry classified as hazardous materials?
Check only one. ☐ Frequently ☐ Sometimes
☐ Seldom or Never

6. If you are driving a company truck, how would you evaluate the company's attitude toward your welfare and working conditions?
Check only one. ☐ Very concerned
☐ Reasonably concerned ☐ Some interest, but not consistent
☐ Has no concern ☐ Does not apply

III. ABOUT YOUR EQUIPMENT

1. Do you own your own truck: ☐ Yes ☐ No
2. If you own a truck, what year is it: 19_____
3. Does the truck you drive have a sleeper cab? ☐ Yes ☐ No
4. Do you own your own trailer? ☐ Yes ☐ No
5. What year is the trailer you pull? 19_____
6. What one type of trailer do you most frequently pull? Check only one. ☐ Van ☐ Tank ☐ Open Top ☐ Reefer ☐ Flat bed ☐ Moving van ☐ Hopper ☐ Dump ☐ Special, other
7. How would you rate the overall condition of the equipment you drive from day to day?

Tractor	Poor or Unsafe	Safe
a. Tires	☐	☐
b. Electrical, lights, signals	☐	☐
c. Brakes	☐	☐
d. Engine	☐	☐
e. Suspension	☐	☐
f. Other	☐	☐

Trailer	Poor or Unsafe	Safe
g. Tires	☐	☐
h. Electrical, lights	☐	☐
i. Brakes	☐	☐
j. Suspension	☐	☐
k. Other	☐	☐

8. Do you report all mechanical and/or safety defects to whomever is responsible for maintaining the equipment? Check only one.
☐ I am personally responsible ☐ Yes, always ☐ Yes, usually ☐ Only if it is really bad ☐ Why bother, they won't fix it anyway.

9. If you ever gave up operating your own truck in the past, what was the main reason? Check only one. ☐ Does not apply
☐ Hassle ☐ Loss of interest in being an owner operator
☐ Mechanical problems ☐ Lack of business ☐ Financial
☐ Other_____

IV. DRIVING AND WORK CONDITIONS

1. There are some aspects of being a truck driver which some people feel make their job difficult.
Please answer the following by checking only one box on each line.

	Does Not Affect Me	Some Difficulty	Major Problem
Cab			
a. Noise	☐	☐	☐
b. Vibration	☐	☐	☐
c. Fumes	☐	☐	☐
d. Seating	☐	☐	
e. Temperature/ Humidity	☐	☐	☐
f. Cleanliness	☐	☐	☐
On the Road			
g. Monotony/ Boredom	☐	☐	☐
h. Loneliness	☐	☐	☐
i. Road conditions	☐	☐	☐
j. Bad weather	☐	☐	☐
k. Night driving	☐	☐	☐
l. Other drivers	☐	☐	☐
m. Federal and state inspections	☐	☐	☐
n. Long driving hours	☐	☐	☐
o. Responsibility for cargo	☐	☐	☐
p. Loading/ unloading cargo	☐	☐	☐
q. Finding loads	☐	☐	☐
r. Unreasonable dispatches, schedules, expectations	☐	☐	☐
Personal			
s. Separation from home	☐	☐	☐
t. Lack of exercise	☐	☐	☐
u. Irregular hours	☐	☐	☐

2. Have you ever used narcotics (such as heroin, opium, cocaine, or codiene) with or without a doctor's prescription just before or while driving during the past year? Check only one.
☐ Never ☐ Once or twice ☐ Occasionally ☐ Regularly

3. Have you ever smoked marijuana (pot) just before or while driving during the past year? Check only one. ☐ Never
☐ Once or twice ☐ Occasionally ☐ Regularly

4. How many hours do you wait to drive after having any alcoholic beverages such as beer, wine, or whiskey? Check only one. ☐ I do not drink ☐ I can drive satisfactorily without waiting. ☐ I wait about 1 hour ☐ I wait about 2 hours ☐ I wait about 3 hours ☐ I wait about 4 hours or more

5. Have you ever used pep pills (bennies, goof-balls, co-pilots, etc.) just before or while driving during the past year? ☐ Never
☐ Once or twice ☐ Occasionally ☐ Regularly

6. How often have you found yourself dozing or falling asleep at the wheel during the past year? ☐ Never ☐ Once or twice
☐ Occasionally ☐ Regularly

– 2 –

Figure B-1 continued

7. How effective have you found the following for staying alert?

Have tried it and find it to be:

	Have never tried it	Not Effective	Effective
a. Stopping, getting out and walking or stretching	☐	☐	☐
b. Wash face with cold water	☐	☐	☐
c. Open the window to get cold air in the face	☐	☐	☐
d. Listen to AM or FM radio or tape deck	☐	☐	☐
e. Listen and/or talk on C.B. radio	☐	☐	☐
f. Refreshment (e.g. coffee, tea, soft drink)	☐	☐	☐
h. Chew gum or tobacco	☐	☐	☐
i. Smoke (cigarettes, cigars, pipe)	☐	☐	☐
j. Sing or talk	☐	☐	☐
k. Change seat position	☐	☐	☐
l. Take "no doze" or other nonprescription stimulant	☐	☐	☐
m. Take amphetamines (i.e., "bennies," "speed," "co-pilots")	☐	☐	☐

8. What speed do you normally cruise at?_____ miles per hour.

9. How often do you stop your truck to rest? About every _____ hours.

10. When you are on the road, where do you usually sleep when you are too tired to drive? Check only one. ☐ Do not sleep on my runs ☐ In sleeper cab ☐ In seat of cab ☐ In motel or hotel ☐ In rest station ☐ On ground on the side of the road ☐ Other_____

11. Do you drive beyond the allowable 10 hours, except on permitted emergencies? Check only one. ☐ Never ☐ Once or twice ☐ Occasionally ☐ Regularly

12. Reasons for you working past allowable driving hours.
a. ☐ Did not work past allowable hours
b. ☐ Unrealistic schedules
c. ☐ Bad weather
d. ☐ Road conditions or detours
e. ☐ Break downs
f. ☐ Stopping to eat or rest
g. ☐ Needed the money
h. ☐ Instructed to by a dispatcher or shipper
i. ☐ Other_____

13. How do you report hours in your log book? Check only one.
☐ Honestly, no matter what
☐ Occasionally misrepresent
☐ Regularly misrepresent
☐ Not sure if correct because I don't really understand the regulations.

14. Do you keep more than one log book?
☐ Yes ☐ No

15. What is your typical (7-day) work week (driving and on duty?)
_____ hours

V. HOW ARE YOU PAID?

1. How are you *typically* paid? Check only one.
☐ Percent of revenue ☐ Hourly wage
☐ By the mile ☐ Other

2. Do you have a source of income outside of driving?
☐ Yes ☐ Sometimes ☐ No

3. Do you have to pay your own traffic violations?
☐ Yes ☐ Sometimes ☐ No

4. Do you have to pay your own over-weight violations?
☐ Yes ☐ Sometimes ☐ No

5. Do you have to pay your own hotel or motel expenses on the road? ☐ Yes ☐ Sometimes ☐ No

6. Did your driving income provide a "good living" this past year?
☐ Yes ☐ Not sure ☐ No

7. How much more income would you require to provide a "good living" (0 if no more)?
a. About _____ percent
b. $ _____ per year

VI. QUESTIONS FOR OWNER OPERATORS

1. Are you an owner operator? Check only one.
a. ☐ No – If this is your answer, do not answer the rest of the questions.
b. ☐ Yes – driving for myself most of the time.
c. ☐ Yes – leased to another carrier most of the time on trip leases.
d. ☐ Yes – leased to another carrier most of the time on leases that may be canceled with 30 day notice.

2. How do you feel about being an owner operator? Check only one. a. ☐ Fine. Plan to replace my current equipment when this wears out.
b. ☐ Want to continue only until this equipment wears out, but will *not* replace it.
c. ☐ Want to get out as soon as possible.

3. What factors contribute to the economic problems of owner operators in your category? a. ☐ Not a problem – or b. ☐ Rates too low c. ☐ Owner operators paid too small portion of rates d. ☐ Too many owner operators competing for the same business e. ☐ Unexpected costs f. ☐ Poor financial management g. ☐ Restrictive safety regulations h. ☐ I.C.C. regulations and authorities i. ☐ Other_____

4. There are reports of owner operators experiencing problems working with contractors, brokers, and companies. Please answer the following by checking only one box in each row based on your own experience.

	No Problem	Problem	Major Problem
a. Unauthorized deductions	☐	☐	☐
b. Slow pay	☐	☐	☐
c. Carrier cutting rates	☐	☐	☐
d. Holdbacks	☐	☐	☐
e. Not paid in full	☐	☐	☐
f. Finance charge deductions	☐	☐	☐
g. No or false rated freight bills	☐	☐	☐
h. Other Problems	☐	☐	☐

– 3 –

Figure B-1 continued

5. Does the company you pull for require the following from you? Check one on each line.

	Yes	No	Does Not Apply
a. Escrow fund deposit	☐	☐	☐
b. Fuel purchased from the company at prices above what you would pay elsewhere	☐	☐	☐
c. Insurance from the company above what you would pay elsewhere	☐	☐	☐
d. Road taxes	☐	☐	☐

6. What is your status on payments on your equipment?
☐ Current (within a month)   ☐ Late (1-2 months behind)
☐ Over 2 months late   ☐ Does not apply

7. Who arranges your back hauls?   ☐ Broker   ☐ Myself
☐ Agent   ☐ Company personnel   ☐ Other

Please return to:

D. Daryl Wyckoff
Post Office Box 461
Marblehead, MA 01945

Please use this space for any additional comments you would like to make.

_____

_____

_____

_____

_____

_____

_____

_____

_____

_____

_____

_____

_____

_____

– 4 –

Figure B-1 continued

Table B–1
Sample Size, DRVRS Data Base,
Indicating Labor Status and Type of Operation

| Labor Status | Type of Operation | | |
	Owner-Operator	Company Drivers	Not Specified
Union	1,017	6,532	267
Nonunion	888	745	131
Not specified	23	20	7

Total sample = 9,630 drivers.

Table B–2
Sample Size, DRVRS Data Base,
Indicating Regulatory Status and Type of Operation

| Regulatory Status | Type of Operation | | |
	Owner-Operator	Company Drivers	Not Specified
Exempt	100	89	15
Private	46	432	21
Contract	599	483	81
Common	710	5,860	213
Other	311	146	36
Not specified	162	287	39

Total sample = 9,630 drivers.

Table B–3
Sample Size, DRVRS Data Base,
Indicating Sex of Driver

Sex of Driver	
Male	9,540
Female	57
Not specified	33

Total sample = 9,630 drivers.

Index

Index

About the Author

D. Daryl Wyckoff is a professor at the Harvard University Graduate School of Business Administration, George F. Baker Foundation. He received the B.S. in aeronautical engineering from M.I.T., the M.B.A. from the University of Southern California, and the D.B.A. from Harvard University. In the past he has served as vice president of the logistics systems group of a California-based aerospace conglomerate and has been the manager of an interstate motor carrier. He continues to serve as a consultant in management, transportation, and logistics to companies, governments, and industrial organizations in the United States, United Kingdom, and several countries in the Orient and the Middle East. Professor Wyckoff is the author of *Organizational Formality and Performance in the Motor Carrier Industry* (Lexington Books, 1974) and *Railroad Management* (Lexington Books, 1975), and coauthor of *The Owner-Operator: Independent Trucker* (Lexington Books, 1975), *The Motor-Carrier Industry* (Lexington Books, 1977), *The Domestic Airline Industry* (Lexington Books, 1977), *The Chain-Restaurant Industry* (Lexington Books, 1978), and *Operations Management: Text and Cases* (Richard D. Irwin, 1975). His articles have appeared in *Traffic World, Modern Railroads, Handling and Shipping, Transportation and Distribution Management,* and *Transport Topics.*